Behind The Mask

What Michael Jackson's
Body Language Told The World

D1516983

Craig James Baxter

Catherine Van Tighem (Siren) is a self-taught artist who has been sketching since early childhood. Inspired by the talent, dedication, and pursuit of excellence set by one of the greatest artists and humanitarians of all time, Michael Jackson, she now uses her art to help contribute to his dream of healing the world. You can see more of her work at her website: mjartbysiren.com

Finally, I would like to thank my beautiful partner, Kat Whitley, because as you can imagine, writing a book takes up a lot of time - time which was spent away from her. I need to thank her for supporting me throughout the compiling of this book - I promise I will take you to New York to compensate you for my absence. This book has taught me a valuable lesson, which is never to lose sight of what's truly important in life - your loved ones.

Behind The Mask

What Michael Jackson's
Body Language Told The World

Contents

Introduction

Michael Jackson was considered by many to be the greatest performer the world has ever seen; his music and performances made him one of the most famous and iconic individuals to ever grace the stage. However, great success often comes with great anguish. When people think back to Michael Jackson, most will remember his music and legendary dance routines, but his well-documented private life and the sordid and often damning allegations against him have cast a dark shadow which I am hoping to address in this book.

Body language is such an integral part of our daily lives, but more often than not we are completely oblivious to the silent messages that we are both sending out and receiving from others. Right now for instance, as you read this book, you will have adopted a stance or posture which is comfortable depending on the circumstances of your location – for example, you may be displaying a closed posture if you are uncomfortable with the proximity of a person near you. Eminent body language expert and zoologist Desmond Morris states that '...*we all carry with us, everywhere we go, a port-*

able territory called a personal space. If people move inside this space, we feel threatened' (Morris, 2002: 192). This stance or posture which you have arrived at will have probably been molded for years, and you will almost certainly have no inclination as to where it originated from, or why you decided on such an action. Granted that this is just a trivial example of how we get into repeated behavioral patterns, but these actions make our daily routines detectable, and we can also apply the same logic to other aspects of everyday behavioral actions.

When we talk about body language, it's often said that we are all different, however in contrast to this statement, we are all actually the same, anatomically speaking. The popular school of thought (as championed by Darwin back in 1859) is that we all descend from a species of primate called Homosapiens, which is essentially responsible for our same basic bodily structure: two arms, two legs, two eyes and so on.   Morris elaborates upon this in his book The Human Animal when he states that *'everything we do has an inborn genetic basis and all our activities have something in common with other species.   Uniquely however, we have built on these animal patterns, exaggerating and elaborating them to an amazing degree and sometimes suppressing them with damaging consequences'* (Morris, 1994:6)

Our fundamental behavior has not deferred much from that of our primitive ancestors. Despite the fact that we might adapt and absorb mannerisms & idiosyncrasies from our families, friends and superiors which make our personalities unique, watch one person and then another and soon you will realize that the behaviors we perform are remarkably similar, and are as predictable as those we are watching. As Morris highlights *'despite the many fascinating variations that exist from region to region and society to society, every one of the millions of human beings alive today shares an almost identical genetic inheritance'* (Morris, 1994: 6).

I undertook this body language project not knowing what I might find. I have been studying non-verbal communication for the past 8 years, and have a thorough knowledge of the human body and its limitless actions. My years of study in anatomy, physiology and emotions have helped me to develop an understanding of common, subtle and micro behavioral movements and the silent messages they send out. I decided to focus on Michael Jackson's body language specifically because he was such a world-famous figure who was, in my opinion, subject to some unfair and perhaps unfounded accusations regarding his private life.

I hope you will believe me when I say that the observations that you are about to read in this book are not biased or influenced in any way. I, like many people, am a fan of Michael's music, however I don't allow my musical preferences to dictate any sort of bias towards Michael Jackson, or this book. My observations are based on years of research and study, and nothing more. Also, despite the fact that I have researched most of the key facts surrounding the cases which I'm behaviorally dissecting, many Michael Jackson fans know his private life in great detail - I do not. I feel that this actually gives me an advantage in writing this book, as I'm unaware of some of the myths and mis-truths associated with Michael. I wrote this book with two objectives in mind: firstly, to decipher what Michael Jackson's body language showed the world, and secondly, to educate you, the reader, on how our often very subtle body language movements reveal our true feelings and sentiments.

So this brings me on to Michael Jackson, who was fundamentally no different to you or I. Granted, I didn't know Michael personally, yet I am confident that the ones who knew him best would state that he indeed had the same strengths, weaknesses and fragilities that we all share as a race. Before I begin the analyses, I need to highlight a few key points about observing body language. Firstly, it is of paramount importance (in order to become truly adept in reading body language) to be able to understand the postures, expressions, gestures, movements and idiosyncrasies of the person whom you are analyzing. This form of research is essential because you need to formulate what is known as 'baseline behavior'. Former FBI Agent and bestselling body language author Joe Navarro states the importance of baselines in his book 'What Every Body Is Saying', as he emphasizes that "*by examining what's normal, we begin to recognize and identify what's abnormal*" (Navarro, 2008:12).

Establishing a baseline is the holy grail of body language observations; these are your reference points which you use to confidently predict behavior. Establishing a baseline gives body language observers like me an opportunity to become familiar with repeated chains of movements and emotional responses. These enable the observer to draw a more accurate conclusion about a person's behavior and make it slightly easier to undertake judgment calls. As I have previously mentioned, we all get into behavioral patterns that are comfortable, and these precise actions are the ones which make up our unique mannerisms and idiosyncrasies. These behaviors take years to perfect, and as such, they form part of our subconscious, meaning these displays are performed without awareness, prompts or any other conscious thought. I never met Michael Jackson, however as I was growing up in the 80s and 90s, many aspects of his life were well-documented and broadcast on every single medium available at the time. Because every aspect of Michael Jackson's life was captured, these recordings enabled me to examine his behavioral style and allowed me to gain a good understanding of both his verbal and non-verbal repertoire. There is a sad irony about this book, because as you delve further into my insights, Michael states repeatedly that the mass media made his life a "*nightmare*"; however if it wasn't for this level of media scrutiny, this book wouldn't have been possible.

The second point I need to highlight is the importance of universal behaviors. These are behaviors which carry the same meaning regardless of ethnicity, age, race, culture, nationality, gender, religion and so on. Having a firm understanding of someone's 'unique' and universal behaviors will enable the observer to correctly identify the meanings behind our bodily displays with a higher degree of accuracy than those who are unaware of their importance. Another aspect which demonstrates the importance of our universal behaviors is that they appear no matter how your demeanor is portrayed. I feel that this is especially important during this topic, because as I've stated, Michael made no secret of the fact that the media often portrayed him to be something he wasn't. Such is the power of the media, television companies can edit segments of film to make someone look gloriously wonderful, or distinctly suspicious. For instance, the interview that British journalist Martin Bashir did with Michael in 2003 entitled Living with Michael Jackson (which I will later analyze in detail in chapter four) could be argued as being an example of yellow journalism, meaning that it was deliberately sensationalist and edited in a biased way.

This type of selective editing can be seen in reality television shows around the world, where editors manipulate 'real time' footage to alter the viewers' perception of the contestants. If all the contestants in the show were shy, reclusive introverts, no-one would watch, so distorting footage to create issues that aren't really there can often increase the show's viewing figures. The same applies to Michael Jackson's life - to quote the title of a book by Eric Bischoff: Controversy Creates Cash (2006). If the mass media decided to portray Michael Jackson in a controversial or unfavorable light (knowing full well that this approach would generate more revenue through sales), then the public's impression of him would change in the blink of an eye. Michael was fully aware of this media sabotage, and stated more than once in different interviews that *"If people hear a lie long enough, people believe it."* The clever use of editing during any interview can create a smokescreen, one in which the messages trying to be delivered (either verbally or silently) are distorted, and the truth remains hidden. Sadly, this scenario could have occurred during some of Michael's interviews. However, understanding universal behaviors as well as baseline patterns is one way around this media manipulation.

Also, this book will help you to become familiar with Michael's life. You will no doubt learn things that you never knew about Michael, and in the process, you may notice the actions and gestures he showed when observing your friends, families and co-workers. I have also included a body language terminology section at the end of the book so you can familiarize yourself with some of the terms I will use in this book.

Here follows my detailed analyses of 5 Michael Jackson interviews in chronological order.

The Oprah Winfrey Interview 1993

In my opening analysis of Michael Jackson, I will review footage of his 1993 interview with Oprah Winfrey filmed at Michael's Neverland Ranch.

This interview was filmed on 10th February 1993 and was the first Michael had given in 14 years. It is reported that this interview was watched by over 90 million viewers in the US, making it one of the most watched TV programs ever. Because this was Michael's first television interview in years, it gave me an opportunity to develop an insight into his personality, demeanor, movements and behavioral style. This interview doesn't appear to have been edited in any way. Please note that I am covering the interview to assess Michael Jackson's body language, so as such I will only be covering certain aspects of this interview (mainly just the moments that are significant). This interview was filmed 6 months before any sexual abuse allegations came to light.

The interview starts with Oprah Winfrey introducing Michael, who proceeds to walk towards her. Their initial greeting is performed with a very soft handshake initially offered by Oprah, and Michael further extends the greeting by giving Oprah a kiss on her cheek. Before Michael has the opportunity to take his seat, Oprah bluntly asks him *"How nervous are you right now?"* Michael takes his seat, and looks distinctly flustered. He responds by saying *"How what?"* It is very unlikely that he did not hear the question, as the room was silent and he made eye contact with Oprah when she spoke. This type of avoidance can be prevalent when someone hasn't had enough time to formulate an answer due to being caught unawares. Michael was probably embarrassed about the abruptness of this question during their opening salutation display.

Our salutation (greeting) displays are a vital aspect of everyday relations. Our greeting rituals depend on numerous factors, such as the relationship with our greeter, the time since the last meeting and the location of the greeting. As a general rule, we greet old friends differently than people whom we have just met, and you would greet those people differently than you would your boss. I am unaware if Michael and Oprah had met prior to this interview; however the lack of initial friendliness shown by Oprah towards Michael, in his own house, filled me with concern about the tone the interview might subsequently take. Often the old adage of '*getting off on the wrong foot*' can be attributed to a lack of rapport, either verbally or non-verbally, during the greeting display.

Michael now answers the original question and states that he never gets nervous, however he tightens his lips in the process, which is a contradictory gesture. This body language behavior can be seen when someone is experiencing discomfort, and this immediate silent response from Michael tells me that he wasn't quite expecting to be made to feel so uncomfortable in his own home within the first few seconds of the interview. Tightening of the lips is a classic universal behavior, often performed out of frustration or nerves.

Oprah continues and says that Michael had stated that he was willing to talk about everything, and that they hadn't discussed a single question prior to recording. Michael's immediate response to this was to remove the cushion from behind his back (placing it on the floor at the side of him) and subsequently he adjusts his posture to a more upright one. This behavior is quite significant as it would appear that Michael is consciously adopting a stronger posture than before. Perhaps the initial lack of rapport-building between the two has shifted Michael's demeanor from him believing this to be a relatively relaxed interview, to it becoming a more confrontational one. Posture shifts such as this one might seem innocuous during our daily lives, however they often carry a very significant message to the receiver.

The camera angle then gives us a whole body shot of Michael, who since adjusting his posture has now adopted a leg barrier. This is quite significant behavior according to zoologist Desmond Morris, who has stated that our feet communicate exactly what we think and feel more honestly than other parts of our bodies (Morris, 1985, 244). This leg barrier is performed by crossing one leg over the other in front of someone, creating a subconscious block against something we dislike. "*All forms of leg-crossing provide a leg-to-leg self-intimacy in which one limb-surface feels the comforting pressure of the other. Clamping one leg firmly around the other can increase this sensation and is a sure sign of someone needing comfort.*" (Morris 2002, 145) What stood out is how this behavior corresponds with Michael's previous displays. He silently revealed his frustration by tightening his lips and adopting a postural change, and now he has performed a leg barrier directed at

Oprah. Having just witnessed these three revealing behaviors, I was beginning to have serious concerns about the non-verbal displays being shown by Michael, as he was using clusters of behaviors associated with frustration. I believe he will have shown these behavioral clusters due to his discomfort at the direct questions being asked by Oprah.

Oprah then asks Michael *"Were you as happy off stage as you appear to be on stage?"*, and he responds by stating that when he is on stage, its feels like *"home"* but once he gets off stage, he is very lonely and sad. He further describes that often during his childhood, he cried from loneliness. Michael then states that the price of fame is almost like a double-edged sword, stating that on one side he gets to travel the world, meet new people and go places, however there is another side to fame. Upon making this switch, he says *'not that I'm complaining'* and at the same time, makes what's known as an 'emblematic gesture'. The gesture that Michael uses replicates the action of stop, which is performed by placing the hand in front of the body, palm facing up, so that the message is visible to the receiver. For a visual aid regarding this gesture, think of a policeman silently stopping traffic in the street. It is as though he wanted to reinforce the fact that he isn't complaining about the downside of fame. Pioneering facial expert Dr Paul Ekman states that *"emblems have a very precise meaning, known to everyone within a cultural group. Most emblems are performed right out in front of the person, between the waist and the neck area. An emblem can't be missed when it is in the presentation position."* (1985, 103)

Michael continues and states that the rehearsals take a lot of your time when you are famous, which he corresponds by making two very distinct hand gestures. The first action comes when Michael says *'your time'* – his hand sweeps towards his heart, which gives the impression that the time needed to practise must come from here, and the best way to transmit this message is to bring the hand towards the heart to demonstrate the importance. The second action is made directly after this display, where Michael clenches his fist when stating that he has to give up his time to rehearse. This hand tightening display is often used to emphasize one's efforts to achieve something, because as Morris says, if someone is making a powerful point, they may clench their fist as if about to punch an invisible opponent (1994: 13). The fist gesture plays a crucial role in non-verbal communication, as it nearly always represents power, and Michael's subconscious use of his fist emphasizes the importance of his words.

Michael continues and talks about the impact fame had on his childhood. He states that he didn't have any friends when he was little, and tells Oprah that the reason he frequently has children around him is that he's compensating for his lack of a childhood. For the first time in this interview, Michael can be seen smiling. Oprah tells him that many people consider him to be an "old soul in a little body" and he responds by saying that when he was little, he was referred to as a *"45 year old midget"* and he makes a repeat of the fist gesture. This is an example of how we get into repeated behavior movements and gestures. Michael has favored the fist action twice during this interview and it forms part of his silent communication repertoire in order to add weight to pertinent words or ideas in his statements.

Oprah then asked for his opinion about his sister's La Toya's book - La Toya: Growing Up in the Jackson Family, in which she directly accused their father of physical and mental abuse during their childhood. When Oprah directly asks Michael *'do you feel that some of the things that she's been say-*

ing are true?' he replies by saying '*I couldn't answer, Oprah, I…*
honestly… I haven't read the book, that's the honest truth'. At the
start of this reply, he rotates his hands, which is a gesture
often performed when we genuinely don't know the answer
to something, Then, just before he says the word '*honestly*',
he again uses the stop emblem to emphasize that he really
doesn't know what the content of the book is, and also, he is
wanting to actually stop Oprah's direct line of questioning
on what appears to be a very difficult topic for him.

Next, when Oprah asks him '*so there was nobody for you to play
with other than your brothers, you never had slumber parties?'*, Michael interrupts her by replying '*never*' and gives a blocking
arm gesture at the same time, implying that this question
makes him feel uncomfortable. "*People feel safer behind some
kind of physical barrier. If a social situation is in any way threatening,
then there is an immediate urge to set up such a barricade.*" (Morris,
2002: 197)

Oprah then asks Michael what it was like during his adolescence and he replies that it was very difficult, as he had to
cope with his fame. Michael says that he used to have terrible pimples (blotches) which meant that he had to wash his

face in the dark because he was embarrassed. He continues and confesses that his father, Joseph Jackson, called him ugly because of his pimples, and he issues an apology to his father ('sorry Joseph') for revealing this. This confession was accompanied by a nervous smile, as if expecting a repercussion from that statement. Interestingly, he refers to his father not as Dad, but as Joseph, which is a classic example of distancing language (this is especially prevalent when we wish to detach ourselves from a person or situation). Michael further discussed how he was expected to address his father in the Martin Bashir interview that I will cover in Chapter Four.

Michael continues and says that he would cry every day about his facial appearance. He tells Oprah that he loves his father, but doesn't know him; she then asks he if he's angry with his father for calling him ugly, and he mirrors the question back to her (*"am I angry with him?"*). As previously mentioned, often when we are asked a question that we weren't prepared for, we repeat the question to give ourselves a fraction longer to think about our answer. Also, when he is formulating in his mind an answer to this question, he looks down a lot (which is an evasive action) because this is a difficult and uncomfortable line of questioning for him.

Michael's initial response is a very distinct gesture when asked the question '*let's talk about these (last) 10 years – is that when you started to go inside yourself because obviously you haven't spoken to any of us... to the world?*' Before replying verbally, he noticeably shifts his posture and bends and lifts his right leg so that the ankle sits just above the knee of the left leg. He then further emphasizes his discomfort when he grabs his right leg with both hands and pulls it towards him, therefore giving him added security. The significance of having his leg now across his body is that it forms a physical barrier between him and Oprah, which further demonstrates how uncomfortable he is with the prying questions she is asking. The leg barrier is something you will no doubt see throughout your daily life, and is performed in a number of different ways depending upon the person's mood, leg flexibility and the social setting.

Next, Oprah asks Michael if his father ever beat him and before he has time to give his answer, his lips tighten once more. This behavior again demonstrates the notion that our facial expressions work faster than our words do. These minute expressions are known as micro-expressions, which as Ekman (1985:129) explains *'provide a full picture of the concealed emotion, but so quickly that it is usually missed. A micro expression flashes on and off the face in less than one quarter of a second.'* Michael's initial silent response was to hide the lips, which is a facial action often linked with concealment. Michael continues and says that his father was a strict disciplinarian and corresponds this by making a fist gesture with his right hand. Michael has shown this hand action previously in this interview, however the message he wishes to send now is significantly more aggressive compared with previous uses. This fist action replicates the action of being hit, which corresponds to Michael's tone. He also amplifies the importance of this silent display by tightening his eyebrows, eyelids and jaw, thus making a facial expression that reinforces the strength of his words.

Michael goes on and states that he was very frightened of his father, so much so that he was physically sick on some occasions when his father came to see him, both as a child and (more worryingly) as an adult. The camera then pans to Oprah, who states that *"everybody has to take responsibility for what they've done in life*", in reference to Michael's abusive father. Oprah here uses a steepling gesture throughout that statement, a gesture that she has used frequently in this interview. Joe Navarro in his book What Every Body Is Saying gives a description of the steepling gesture by saying that it *"involves touching the spread fingertips of both hands, in a gesture similar to "praying hands", but the fingers are not interlocked and the palms may not be touching. It is called steepling because the hands look like the pointed top of a church steeple."* (Navarro, 2008, 147). This gesture is often used to display our confidence, or to enlighten. Overuse of this gesture can send out a message of smugness and pompousness, stating non-verbally 'I am superior" to the receiver. Oprah uses the steepling gesture to showcase her wisdom based on her years of experience at conducting interviews.

Michael again reiterates that he loves his father and that Michael is a forgiving person, however Oprah interrupts him mid-speech, bluntly asking if he can really forgive his father if he hasn't dealt with how he really feels. Michael here looks visually stunned at Oprah's rudeness, which is then acutely revealed as the camera pans round making Michael's full posture visible. He is still shown to be making the very distinct leg barrier towards Oprah as mentioned earlier, which carries the very significant message of '*I wish to block your questions as they are causing me great discomfort and distress.*'

Michael continues and states that there has been a lot of "*garbage*" written about him which are complete lies, and he uses his facial muscles to transmit his anger towards the media who devise these lies. Michael emphatically states that the more times you hear a lie, the more inclined you are to believe it. Oprah then brings out a sheet of paper which contains some questions for Michael to answer so he can set the record straight. The camera angle changes and we are able to see that he has undone his previous leg barrier, however has now adopted a wrist hold to match his still-crossed legs. The wrist hold is performed by placing one hand over the wrist of the opposing arm and is another display often performed when anxiety is present. Michael again is making a double barrier towards Oprah, using the arms and legs as defensive tools. One could suggest that the lack of rapport between Oprah and Michael is causing him to close himself off, which could make the remainder of the interview problematic.

Next, Oprah asks Michael about the '*oxygen chamber rumor*', and proceeds to show a picture of him in a glass structure (the rumor at the time was that Michael slept in an oxygen chamber because he didn't want to grow old.) Michael states that the reason he was in this structure was that he was badly burned whilst filming a commercial for Pepsi and the money he was awarded in compensation was used to create the Michael Jackson Burns Centre, and the apparatus he is pictured in is in fact used for burns' victims during their treatment. While Michael seeks to set the record straight about this rumor, his hands make a series of gesticulations (such as finger pointing) which compliment his words. These are examples of '*illustrators*' which help the receiver (Oprah) gain a better understanding of the verbal message. Dr. Paul Ekman wrote the following about 'illustrators' in his 1985 book 'Telling Lies':

"*Illustrators are called by that name because they illustrate speech as it is spoken. There are many ways to do so: emphasis can be given to a word or phrase, much like an accent mark or underlining; the flow of thought can be traced in the air, as if the speaker is conducting her speech; the hands can draw a picture in a space or show an action repeating or amplifying what is being said. It is the hands that usually illustrate speech, although brow and upper eyelid movements often pro-vide emphasis illustrators, and the entire body or upper trunk can do so also"* (Ekman, 1985, 104-105)

Regarding the oxygen chamber rumour, Michael then angrily states that no-one should pass judgment on anyone unless they have spoken with that person one on one, and he makes a series of angered finger-point gestures to emphasize his fury. Pointing the finger carries with it a very precise meaning and target, which in this case is the media for print-ing these lies that Michael is having to redress. His anger and frustration at the media's false reporting of him is further emphasized by his use of a chopping action with his hand. The camera pans back to Michael's posture and he has again resumed the double arm/leg barrier towards Oprah. He is resorting to postures that he feels comfortable with, and these barriers are helping him to deal with Oprah's probing and difficult questions.

Oprah continues by referring to her list of questions, and asks Michael if he had bought The Elephant Man's bones (the Elephant Man was actually an English man called Jo-seph Merrick born in 1862 who had a severe facial deformity which made him resemble an elephant). He verbally denies this rumor, however he does tell her that he can relate to The Elephant Man's story, but laughs off the reports that he bought his bones. Michael further reiterates that if you hear a lie long enough, people will believe it. Next, Oprah asks Michael if the story about him wanting a little white boy to play him in a Pepsi commercial was true. Michael emphatically denies this "*horrifying*" rumor and juts his head forwards in time to his denials. He continues and tells Oprah that the face in the commercial was his face as a child and states that he's proud to be a black American; he places his open palm across his chest to add intensity to this statement. Michael also states that he has a lot of dignity and makes a repeat of the fist gesture (already seen during this interview) in order to give weight to his argument about these accusations being false. He then showcases his anger at this allegation by thrusting his finger at Oprah whilst asking (rhetorically) if she would have an Oriental child play her as a child.

Oprah then proceeds to ask Michael about the color of his skin, and tells him that it is noticeably different from when he was a child. She asks him if his skin is lighter because he doesn't like being black, and if he is bleaching his skin. Michael places his hand on his heart and states that as far as he knows, there is no such thing as '*skin bleaching*', and tells Oprah that he has a skin disorder called vitiligo which destroys the pigmentation of the skin. Michael emphatically denies that the stories about his skin are related to racial issues, and his demeanor instantly changes from anger to sadness. We can see this because his eyes start to fill with tears when he discusses his skin disorder. Michael then reverts back to anger when he states that millions of people sit out in the sun to become darker and to become someone other than themselves. Michael's anger can be seen through his protruding jaw action and his direct finger points towards Oprah. He says that his skin disorder stems from his father's side & reiterates that he's not taken anything to change the color of his skin. Michael also tells Oprah that he uses make-up to even out the blotches on his skin, and he makes a distinct hand movement to mimic the action of spreading it. Again, these hand movements are examples of '*illustrators*' and can often be present during honest statements.

Oprah asks Michael how much plastic surgery he's had, and he responds quickly and without hesitation by saying '*very very little*'. I feel that if he was lying, one would have expected more of a hesitation whilst he formulated a false an-answer, and he may have used more speech disturbances e.g. ums and erms as described by Vrij and Semin (1996:65). He then says that you can count on two fingers how many times he's had plastic surgery, and he replicates this by holding up two fingers. This is an example of something called '*gestural timing*', meaning his words precisely match the body language gesture on show. He then says '*if you want to know about those things* (i.e. plastic surgery)... *all the nosy people in the world... read my book*', but what is interesting here is that when he says '*all the nosy people in the world*' he then follows that with a nervous smile and giggle. This could be attributed to the fact that he is trying to imply that Oprah herself is being nosy by asking this question and he is slightly embarrassed by this. Furthermore, just before he says '*read my book*' she shows her superiority and unfortunate lack of respect for his point of view by interrupting him again, saying '*once we say it, we don't have to say it anymore*' (meaning that she wants Michael to admit there and then to the amount of plastic surgery he's had). Michael goes on to say that "*if every person in Hollywood*

who's had plastic surgery went on holiday, the town would be empty".
The camera pans back to Oprah who reluctantly agrees with
Michael, however she is again making the steepling gesture.
Like I have previously mentioned, overuse of the steepling
gesture can send out the wrong message, making the sender
appear infallible and indeed smug. Oprah (whilst steepling)
asks Michael if he had the plastic surgery because he was
unhappy with how he looked during his younger years. His
immediate response was to roll his eyes before he proceeds
to say *no, not really… its only two things, really …get my book, it's
no big deal.* You can tell by the fact that he uses the com-
mand word *get* that he is running out of patience with
Oprah's demanding line of questioning.

All the body language he demonstrates in this section show
us his increasing frustration at Oprah's questions, because
one could argue that he classes the answers as being private
and personal to him. This again filled me with worry about
the tone this interview was taking. Michael then confirms
that he has had a nose operation, but for the first time in
this interview, he actually interrupts Oprah and states that
he's never had his eyes, cheeks or lips operated on. This
could be another sign of his increasing frustration at her

continual interruptions, so much so that he has decided to turn the tables. He says to Oprah that he never looks in the mirror because he is never pleased by what he sees and again, she is seen to be using the steepling gesture towards him.

Oprah then asks Michael why he grabs his crotch during his performances, and he initially seems embarrassed by this question and laughs nervously, making a partial eye block with his hand. Hiding our eyes with our hands is behavior commonly seen when we suffer embarrassment or disbelief. Again Michael mirrors this question back to Oprah – *"why do I grab my crotch?"* – and his posture immediately switches back to one we have seen previously in this interview, where he crosses his legs and pulls his bent leg towards him for added security. He again makes fist gestures to emphasize that when he hears the bass, he becomes the bass; he then switches his hand gesture into a more slow and deliberate display when he states that when you hear the cello, you become the cello. These silent messages transmit a very distinct change in musical mimicry. Michael states that his crotch grab comes from the music, and is not necessarily a conscious action.

Oprah asks Michael if there is always pressure to do something bigger and better, and he states that he does try to be original and his music comes from the heart, which corresponds with him placing his hand over his heart. Again, this is an example of how our bodily actions supplement the meaning of our words.

The camera then pans wide which makes Michael's seated posture visible. He is still adopting the leg cross position, however this time is making a one sided 'akimbo' gesture with his elbow. "*Arms akimbo is a good way of saying that there are "issues," "things are not good," or "I am standing my ground" in a territorial display*" (Morris, 1985:195). This display further highlights Michael's present discomfort during this interview. Often you will see the arms akimbo gesture when someone is around a person that they dislike, where the arms are used as a barrier to fend off that person from getting too close. Again, this is another common display associated with frustration.

Next, Oprah asks Michael where the term '*King of Pop*' came from, and asked if it was he himself who had coined it. He clutches the fingers of his left hand with his right hand whilst formulating an answer. Navarro (2008) highlights the importance of pacifying behaviors when he says that they are often prevalent when people are not at ease or are reacting negatively to something. Michael states that he's never proclaimed himself to be '*The King Of Pop*' – but in fact Elizabeth Taylor coined the saying '*king of pop, rock and soul*' to describe him during an 1989 awards show and his fans have globally adopted this shortened version.

Michael goes on and tells Oprah that he's currently dating Brooke Shields and that he indeed loves her. Oprah presses him into revealing that he once loved somebody else, but he doesn't disclose her name. Throughout this conversation, Michael reveals his anxiety by making a nervous touch of his ear. Innocuous as this might seem, it is in fact a classic and subconscious reaction to hearing something that we don't like, as the fingers almost want to block out the question by distorting the sound to our ears. This action is called a '*manipulator*' and they are present when we experience a particularly stressful moment. They can take many forms as Ekman outlines, such as when one part of the body '*grooms, massages, rubs, holds, pinches, picks, scratches or otherwise manipulates another part of the body*' (1985:109-110)

Oprah then (quite unbelievably and blatantly) asks Michael if he's a virgin. Michael is so understandably astonished at such an intrusive question that he instinctively places his hands over his eyes to block out the eye contact between the two of them, and giggles in a self-conscious way. Often when we are extremely embarrassed we go to great lengths to avoid eye contact, as for instance, children will often run and hide when they experience something embarrassing. Adults have adapted the barrier, but it has not lost any of its childhood innocence. Michael again makes a tight-lipped facial expression, which as discussed, is a classic indicator of concealed anger. He tries to laugh off this question, and states that he's a gentleman and is embarrassed by it, but his tight lips reveal that he was exceptionally displeased by this abrupt and disrespectful question.

Michael goes on and states that his life wouldn't be complete if he didn't marry or have children as he adores the family life, and he reveals to Oprah that he's always had a crush on Diana Ross since he was a child. When he admits this secret, he breaks eye contact with Oprah, bites his bottom lip slightly and smiles awkwardly – all classic signs of embarrassment. Oprah then asks Michael if he has ever proposed to his friend Elizabeth Taylor; he denies this rumor, but states that he would have liked to have done so.

The follow segment of the footage I feel is the most significant part of this interview, however for all the wrong reasons.

Oprah then introduces Dame Elizabeth Taylor into the interview. After Michael stands to greet Elizabeth, she sits down in the chair that he was using. What happens next is truly remarkable, as he is left standing next to the seated Elizabeth Taylor, in a stance that is very similar to that of a naughty school child who has been dragged into the principal's office to be disciplined (as he has his head bowed and his hands clasped behind his back). This was a huge faux pas on the part of the production team, as this error in the seating arrangements removed all the focus and power from Michael, who now looks distinctly uneasy about being left standing while the other two are seated.

Elizabeth then emphatically states that Michael has indeed never proposed to her, and likewise she has never proposed to him. When she says this, she makes a prolonged gaze towards Michael and smiles warmly, which demonstrates that she has a real fondness towards him (you would not gaze at someone you had just met in this way). As Morris states, this long-looking is a sign of loving behavior (2002:105).

Oprah then asks Elizabeth what is most misunderstood about Michael Jackson, and she states that he's the least *"weird"* man she's ever known; rather he is highly intelligent, shrewd and intuitive. The camera then pans to Michael's face, and he is making a very distinct tightening of his lips. We have seen this behavior from him frequently throughout this interview, however this particular expression was performed with much more intensity than the other examples. One could suggest that his anger at the direct personal questions being asked about his private life and the fact that his status has been removed is beginning to leak out from him. This pronounced example of lip hiding behavior shows a massive increase in frustration on his part. There should have been another chair brought out for Michael to keep everything level and even, yet instead, Michael has lost his status. Because of this error, the questions Oprah asks now seem quite condescending, almost like Michael isn't there. The camera again pans to him, however this time he juts out his jaw - another example of an expression of anger. Michael is again experiencing deep frustration.

Michael again looks increasingly uneasy when Elizabeth talks about their friendship. She states that their childhoods were actually very similar, as she also had an abusive father and both were childhood stars. The camera angle then pans to the back of Michael and Elizabeth, facing Oprah, showing that Michael has placed his hands behind his back. "*Putting the arms behind the back is a clear signal that means, "Don't get close; I don't want to make contact with you*" (Navarro, 2008, 117) Again, this behavior he is displaying corresponds with his recent movements and expressions. Remember that clusters of similar behaviors are needed before making an accurate assessment of someone's mood, and with that in mind, within the last few minutes of this interview, we have seen Michael hide his lips, jut out his jaw and now he has placed his hands behind his back. All of these three gestures carry a very similar message: '*I am very frustrated and neither happy nor comfortable*'.

Oprah then asks Elizabeth what she wants the world to know about Michael Jackson. Immediately after asking this,

Oprah does give away one clue in her body language that *'leaks'* the fact that she is uncomfortable with the seating problem (and perhaps the whole interview itself) – her eyes dart momentarily towards the camera which makes her appear slightly worried. Elizabeth states that Michael is a loving, caring, generous man, and a very funny man (which makes him crack a smile briefly), however his facial expression soon returns to a frustrated one.

The interview returns from a commercial and shows Michael and Oprah in a golf buggy driving towards his Neverland theme park. Oprah asks him if he did this for the children or himself, and he replies that it was for both. He then tells Oprah that every three weeks, he has terminally-ill children come to visit the amusement park through the Make-A-Wish foundation. Next, he proceeds to show Oprah around the park and makes the same *'arms behind the back'* posture as shown moments earlier. However, as well as being a social rejection display, this stance can also be used to show how proud we are of something we've done or created (as Michael is of Neverland) or it can be a humbling display. This again further highlights how our body language needs context to make the message clear, because our behavioral displays do not always send out the same message each time they're used. Michael's use of the arms behind the back stance is quite refreshing to see, because throughout the interview so far, he has been on the receiving end of some tough questions and seating clangers, however his status has been fully restored by the use of this humbling arm display.

Michael and Oprah now walk into an empty theatre at Neverland, and she is seen performing the arms-akimbo posture that Michael himself demonstrated during this interview. This is where the arms are placed on the hips and it sends out a very direct message that there are issues. They both take a seat on the edge of the theatre stage and Michael states that he is trying to imitate Jesus' behavior – he states that seeing disadvantaged children playing in his amusement park fills him with happy tears. With Oprah and Michael not having the structure of proper seats, they now have to assume a posture that is comfortable. It's quite noticeable how far away they have chosen to sit from each other, however Michael rectifies this by sliding next to Oprah, reducing the gap. He might have done this because he was conscious of the earlier lack of rapport between them and he was trying to make amends in his own way.

Michael then shows Oprah how he's installed beds into the side of the theatre so children who are very sick and bedridden can watch the performances. Here he makes a partial arm barrier when he talks about the children who are too sick to be able to sit up, which is again another example of a gesture we make whenever we feel uncomfortable. Michael states that these beds are motorized which enables them to move up and down, so that a child who can't sit up can watch the magic shows and cartoons. He further highlights his discomfort at discussing this subject by once again making a leg barrier, which is further emphasized by pulling his bent leg closer to his body.

Michael tells Oprah that after years of sadness, he is truly happy now, and is proud that he has set up the Heal The World foundation. He continues to tell Oprah that he's got 3 goals – the immunization of children, a big brother/big sister program and a drug abuse program, and that he is going state-to-state to help heal the world. Oprah quizzes Michael about another myth - that his Moonwalk isn't real and is actually a camera trick. In response, he gives her a little background into the origin of the Moonwalk, and states that he has adapted the moves from seeing children dance in the ghetto. Michael then proceeds to give Oprah a demonstration of the Moonwalk which amazes her.

Michael continues and states that he's never satisfied with his performances, and tells Oprah that he cried after he did the Moonwalk for the first time at Motown 25 (a show broadcast in 1983 to commemorate the 25th anniversary of Motown). However, Michael states that it was only after talking to a 12 year old fan after that show who praised his dance moves that he knew that he'd done a good job, because children don't lie. This is another example of Michael's chronic lack of self-confidence which was an issue that affected him his whole life (and many would argue stems from his difficult childhood and adolescent years).

Michael then signs a brief song to Oprah, which she bops along too. Once he finishes his performance, she gives his arm a double hand grasp, done to show her appreciation and gratitude. Also, Oprah lowers her body towards Michael, which is a non-verbal sign of respect (in sharp contrast to her earlier attitude towards him). She then gives him an awkward-looking brief full body hug, which Michael doesn't overly lean into. This behavior is common where you are unsure if making full body contact is appropriate, and you feel the need to break away as soon as possible to avoid upsetting or offending the receiver.

Oprah asks Michael if the rumor about whether he told Bill Clinton that only he could sing at Clinton's inauguration is true, which Michael emphatically denies, calling it "*the most stupidest story I've ever heard*". He makes an emphatic hand thrust to illustrate his denial and he also makes another hand scissor and self touch gesture to emphasize the truth.

Oprah then asks Michael what he wants the world to know about Michael Jackson, and he responds by saying he wants to be known as a great artist, and to be loved wherever he goes. The interview ends with Oprah thanking Michael for this interview, and stating that now the interview is over, she is going to ride the ferris wheel and eat popcorn at Neverland, and she hopes that Michael will teach her the Moonwalk. As she states this, she puts her arm on Michael's and gently pulls him away from the stage, a gesture which could be interpreted as her final show of superiority over him, as yet again it shows that she is dominant over him (much like a teacher leading a child out of the classroom). Oprah says to Michael that this has been fun - Michael responds by saying *"yeah, lots of fun"* whilst he is walking, so there was no opportunity for any body language *'leaks'* in terms of what he really thought about the interview. The credits roll and the program ends.

Summary

To conclude, this interview had more twists and turns than a rollercoaster at Neverland. This was Michael's first interview in 14 years which drew in a huge global audience. As I've stated, it was described as being totally unscripted - no edits, no questions rehearsed, just live action between Oprah and Michael. From a body language point of view, for the vast majority of this interview, Michael closed himself off from Oprah - behavior which showed that he was experiencing discomfort. As I've mentioned, this was his first interview for many years, and it gave me an insight into Michael's basic level of movements, gestures and expressions, including how he interacts with people and reacts to stress. The lack of initial rapport between them resulted in leg barriers from Michael, which are subconscious attempts to block out the questions and the anxiety they cause. He intensified the leg block later in the interview (by bringing his crossed leg closer to his body) when the questions became even more prying, because he almost wished to actually repel what was being asked of him as it was so uncomfortable. Also, by pulling his own leg close to him, he is almost giving himself a type of hug for comfort. As the eminent zoologist Desmond Morris states, the *'feet communicate what we think and feel more honestly than any other part of our bodies'* (Morris, 1985:244) It goes back to the old paradigm of moving towards things we like and moving away from things we don't. As Michael can't literally *'flee'* from this interview, he has to perform blocking behaviors in an attempt to provide some inner security. Some of the topics discussed were very sensitive to Michael, and some might say that Oprah went too far by asking him about his plastic surgery and sex life. The stress of being interviewed for the first time after many years, the lack of friendliness shown from Oprah and the arguable flippancy of some of her replies resulted in Michael making more and more behaviors linked with anxiety. The anxiety manifested into anger at some stages of this interview, as he used lip-hiding behaviors and eye blocking gestures, both of which have a relationship with anger. The fiasco of being left standing while Oprah and Elizabeth were seated and the way they talked like Michael wasn't there just further showcased his distain.

I feel that most of the non-verbal responses Michael showed would have been lost at the time this interview was aired, because in 1993, he was the biggest superstar on earth, and people would have been more interested in what he had to say, not the way he said it. From an interview point of view, it was groundbreaking, because it showcased Michael in a completely different light than had ever been seen before. This was because his previous television appearances were to showcase his ability, either as a singer or dancer, whereas this interview showed a far more human side to Michael. He was shown to have the same fragilities that we all share, which, to the average person, would have been quite humbling. Our perception of the rich and famous is that they are somehow immune from the daily struggles of life, however this interview showed that Michael Jackson, despite his grandeur, was just like you or I. Having a difficult upbringing and a lack of childhood friends are often universal problems that many children have to endure, and are not just reserved for the wealthy. His gestures, expressions and behavioral movements are no different to the ones you will see on a daily basis in all the people you observe. From a body language perspective, you can really see how lonely Michael was, as his somber voice and facial expressions will live long in the memory of whoever watches this interview. I got the impression that Michael wanted to set the record straight about certain myths surrounding him, however Oprah's direct and sometimes probing interview style and the seating faux pas made him close himself off. Michael's whole demeanor in this interview appears very child-like and he was very softly spoken, despite the intrusive questions. How he would have behaved if he was made to feel more at ease will never be known, however the interview did give Michael the chance to dispense with some of the many myths about his private life mainly generated by the tabloid press.

In the months after giving this interview to Oprah Winfrey, Michael was accused by Evan Chandler of sexually abusing his 13 year old son, Jordan Chandler. The following interview is a video statement Michael

issued in order to make an official denial of these accusations.

Michael Jackson's Statement from his Neverland Valley Ranch on December 22, 1993

Michael starts by telling us how he wishes to convey his deepest gratitude for our (his fans) love and support. He states that he's doing well and is strong. Michael here is trying his best to conceal his anger; this is manifested by the tightening of his upper eyelids and jaw as he speaks.

Michael continues and states that there have been many disgusting statements made recently concerning allegations of improper conduct on his part. Moments after he says the word *'disgusting'*, he flashes an eye squint expression to demonstrate non-verbally his revulsion at the accusations leveled against him. Eye squinting or blocking *'takes many forms and can be observed at any tragic event (or if) bad news is being broadcast'* (Navarro, 2008:178). Its purpose is to temporarily block out the visual stimulus we don't wish to see, as it is distressing to us, or it can also be a sign of anger.

He goes on to say that these allegations are totally false, and makes an emphatic correlated head shake in the process. This particular head display corresponds perfectly with the verbal message, which adds intensity to that emphatic denial. Michael then states that he wishes for a speedy end to this horrifying, horrifying experience, which is amplified by the use of repeated language and subtle head shakes, both emphasizing Michael's distress. What is also apparent is that he is attempting to mask his anger when he starts describing what he is accused of, because he flashes a teeth clench (an anger micro expression). As I have previously mentioned, Dr. Ekman developed the term micro expressions to describe *'very fast facial movements lasting less than one fifth of a second (and) are one important source of leakage, revealing an emotion a person is trying to conceal'* (2003: 1A)

Michael continues and states that under advice from his lawyers, he will not respond to all of the false allegations being made against him, stating that he is particularly upset by the handling of this matter by the mass media. Upon making that statement, we see two significant arm displays. The first one is made when Michael says *'handling of this matter'* – his arms rise up and are then thrust forward, keeping his palms down. This arm gesture is shown when someone wishes to subconsciously push way something that is causing them distress. If Michael was to have made the *'palms up gesture'*, it would have looked like he was pleading and asking to be believed. You don't see that here; Michael kept his palms down, which is subconsciously enhancing his denial.

The second arm behavior is shown directly after this palm down display. When Michael says *'incredible, terrible mass media'* he makes the hand scissors gesture. *"The Hand Scissor baton adds a strong flavor of denial or rejection to the mood of the speech. It is as if the speaker is cutting his way through a hostile barrier, negating the opposition by striking it away from him, both to the left and to the right."* (Morris, 2002: 82). The hand scissors display is done by moving the arms and hands across the body, then swiftly moving them away, making a chopping action with the arms that replicates a pair of scissors. This hand gesture is significantly more emphatic and forceful than head shaking and delivers a very precise message.

Michael then further illustrates his anger by making a brief *'eye block'* when talking about how the media have manipulated these allegations and drawn their own conclusions. As already mentioned, eye blocking is done to show our anger or distain towards something. Michael urges people to hear the truth before they label or condemn him, and again makes a subconscious head shake '*no*' when he asks not to be treated like a criminal.

Michael then states that he was forced to submit to a dehumanizing and humiliating inspection of his body by law enforcement, and now, his entire demeanor changes in an instant. Moments before this statement, he was making anger emphatic gestures, however now, sadness is registered on his face. His voice goes from emphatic to solemn (and it appears to falter, showing signs of becoming upset) as he continues and explains that these body searches were conducted for any signs of discolorations, blotting, blotches or any other evidence of a skin color disorder called vitiligo. Michael's demeanor again then switches from the solemn expressions seen when talking about the body searches to anger (brief tensing of the eyelids) when talking about how, if he didn't co-operate with law enforcement, it would be an admission of his guilt at any trial.

Michael continues and states that it was the most humiliating ordeal of his life, and he has to take a deep breath in to continue. He is visibly shaken, and states that no one should have to suffer this indignity, and makes another emphatic arm display made with the left arm only; this is an abbreviated version of the hand scissors gesture seen before. He is literally pushing away the distress this bodily search caused him. Since Michael took that deep breath in, his breathing rate dramatically increased. Immediately after the arm gesture, Michael performs a noticeable gulp after he says the word '*indignity*', which is often performed to moisten the mouth. This is just another example of how, when we are under extreme stress, our sympathetic nervous system raises our bodily functions. This autonomic action increases our breathing rate and decreases our saliva production. As Gordon and Fleisher state '*during sympathetic arousal, functions not important to survival cease. Since digesting food is not important to immediate survival, and salivation, whose function is breaking down and lubricating food entering the body, stops, the mouth becomes dry*' (2006:2).

Research into physiology shows that when the body is under extreme stress, our sympathetic nervous system kicks in, which elevates our bodily functions (heart rate, breathing rate, perspiration). Because of this autonomic response, the demand for oxygen elsewhere dries out the salivary glands, which makes our mouths dry. As an aside, it's interesting to note that back in 100BC, the Chinese used this scientific understanding to gauge someone's innocence or guilt during an investigation. The technique was to have an accused person chew crushed dry rice and ask them to spit it out. If the majority of rice was spat, the person was deemed to be telling the truth, as there was enough saliva present to enable spitting. However if the majority of the rice remained in the mouth (especially in the roof of the mouth) it was deemed that this person was guilty because the mouth wasn't wet enough due to an increase in sympathetic arousal (Gordon and Fleisher 2006, 2). Thankfully behavioral science has come a long way since 100BC.

Michael continues and states that even after he was subjected to these intrusive body searches, the parties involved were still not satisfied and so they wanted to take more pictures, which Michael solemnly states was a horrifying nightmare. He goes on and states emphatically that if this is what he has to endure to prove his innocence (his complete innocence) then so be it. Michael emphasizes this point by repeating the word '*innocence*' twice, and the second time he says it, he accompanies it with a longer than normal blink. This behavior can often be associated with disbelief, as the person is trying to shut out what is troubling them. He also thrusts his head forward to further highlight his point. He makes another emphatic head display soon after this when he again completely denies being guilty of these allegations.

Michael continues and states that if he is guilty of anything, it's of giving all he has to give to help children all over the world. Whilst making this statement, Michael makes a cluster of three anger-based movements. Firstly, he makes an eye block, which is done to highlight his frustration at having to declare that he's *'guilty'* of helping children. Also in this section, he stumbles over his words and makes what's known as a speech hesitation when he says: *'but if I am guilty of anything, it is of giving all that I have.....all that I have to give to help children all over the world'*. This is significant not only because it is one of the only errors in his speech that he makes in an interview that's nearly four minutes long, but also because it gives more credibility to his denials, because a liar would have rehearsed this speech over and over, and would not have stumbled over their words. *'Liars may realize that observers pay attention to their behavioral reactions to judge whether they are lying. Liars therefore may attempt to control their behavior'* (Vrij, 2008: 41).

Secondly, Michael subconsciously juts out his head (possibly done as a defiant gesture towards the media) and thirdly, he demonstrates the uni-lateral hand scissor action we have seen before. This arm action adds emphasis to his words, and is a much stronger and visible action than the eye block or head jut. Reinforcement gestures like this give Michael's verbal denials that added intensity. Again, this head behavior is seen moments after the singular hand scissor gesture is made.

Michael then talks about loving children of all ages and races and how he gains sheer joy from seeing children with innocent and smiling faces. He proceeds and quotes from the bible: *"Suffer little children to come unto me, and forbid them not: for of such is the kingdom of Heaven"*. Michael states that he is not God, but God like. Upon stating this, Michael continues to emphatically deny any wrong doing and shakes his head from side to side, which corresponds to his words '*I am totally innocent of any wrong-doing*'. This just demonstrates how body language interpretation is very subjective, because the shaking of his head when he says the words 'totally innocent' may be regarded by some as reflecting the fact that he is not totally innocent. However, I believe that the wealth of other body language evidence provided by Michael in this interview overwhelmingly speaks for itself regarding his innocence.

He goes on to make another uni-lateral hand scissor gesture when he talks about how all these terrible allegations will be proven false, which again bolsters this statement. To bring the interview to a close, Michael thanks his friends and fans for their support and states that together, we will see this through to the very end.

Summary

Throughout this statement, Michael goes through numerous emotional changes. As I have mentioned, anger is certainly apparent at the start of this interview. Michael uses his eyes and jaw to transmit his frustration towards the media, and his repeated use of the hand scissors action is reassuring. These hand actions carry a very precise meaning, and aren't gestures that can be interpreted any other way; he is literally trying to *'chop' this negativity in half.'* These hand scissor actions again can be referred to as *'illustrators'*, or *'illustrating gestures'* (see the Oprah interview in chapter one for further examples). Ekman offers the following analysis regarding illustrators:

"If a liar has not adequately worked out her line in advance, she also will have to be cautious, carefully considering each word before it is spoken. Deceivers who are not rehearsed, who have had little practice in the particular lie, who failed to anticipate what would be asked or when, will show a decrease in illustrators" (Ekman, 1985, 107)

In my opinion, Michael doesn't show a decrease in illustrators, but rather an increase, plus his hand actions are in perfect synchrony with his words. Often when we try to put on an emotion or *'act out'* a story we know isn't true, our bodily actions are not in synchrony with our words. This is because our words work faster than our gestures do. This *'out of sync'* behavior is not seen here in this interview, as Michael's gestural timing is precise, which further adds weight to his emphatic denials. In my opinion, from the behavior I have discussed in this section, it would appear that Michael Jackson was being wholeheartedly honest during this televised denial and had no guilt to conceal.

Michael Jackson's 1996 Police Interview which (according to the footage) was filmed at 3:29pm on March 1st 1996

Please note that this video I have used is incomplete, because there are missing time sections. For instance, the video begins at 3.13pm but then it jumps to 3.29pm approx 17 seconds in, meaning that we do not know what was said for a period of roughly 15 minutes. There are many more missing time segments throughout this video, therefore demonstrating that it has been subject to selective editing at some point. This further reinforces my point that the media have manipulated the account that Michael has given and we are not allowed access to the whole interview for us to make up our own minds. I must stress that it is unclear who actually edited this video so that it contains only the scenes that it does, and what the purpose of this was.

The clip - purportedly taken from a three-hour video - shows Michael fielding a series of questions from the police regarding a 1996 lawsuit filed against him by former staff members at his Neverland Valley Ranch, who claimed they saw Michael abusing young boys. The topics covered include: the allegations made by Jordan Chandler (whose

65

father, Evan Chandler, accused Michael of sexually abusing Jordan in 1993), his relationships with minors like Macaulay Culkin & Brett Barnes and whether he bleaches his skin.

Interviewer (off camera): *Were you aware that Jordan Chandler, or his family on his behalf, filed a lawsuit against you?*

Michael here leans back into his seat and briefly directs his head and eyes down to the ground. This behavior is called a postural retreat and is shown when we hear things we don't like. Ex-FBI Agent and best-selling author Joe Navarro refers to this behavior as the '*The Torso Lean*' in his 2008 book 'What Every Body Is Saying' meaning that "*the torso will react to perceived dangers by attempting to distance itself from anything stressful or unwanted*" (2008: 86). This discomfort behavior can be traced back to the paradigm of moving towards things we like, and away from things we don't. Michael's postural slump, together with his head and eye behavior, show us that he was aware of the lawsuit and answered yes.

Interviewer: *To your knowledge, Mr. Jackson, were you ever accused of having sexually molested Brett Barnes?*

Michael immediately flashes a blended facial expression of surprise and anguish upon hearing this question, which is instantly recognizable. Pioneering facial expert Dr. Paul Ekman states in his book Emotions Revealed that *"sadness, anger, surprise, fear, disgust, contempt and happiness"* are the seven universally recognized emotions (2003). Michael's eyelids widen into what Navarro calls flashbulb eyes (2008:179) which he states are normally associated with surprise. In my opinion, if Michael had committed such an indecent act, his immediate facial expression wouldn't have necessarily been a surprise/anguish blend. If he was guilty of this allegation, I feel that fear would have been the primary emotion flashed on Michael's face. Fear (which I must reiterate **isn't** shown here) could be flashed for a number of reasons, namely the fear that he had been caught out, the fear of what his fans would think, the fear of how the media would portray him, and the deep fear of the punishment. Fear isn't seen here, so Michael has no reason to experience those negative emotions. What's interesting to note is that surprise and anguish are probably the two emotions you and I would experience in this situation, depending on your personality. Michael was noted for having a quite gentile nature, so the anger that one might also feel about being accused of this indecent allegation doesn't register with him. Another point I feel is worth making is that at no stage does Michael try to conceal or suppress his emotional response to this question.

After his initial emotional non-verbal response to this question, Michael proceeds to place both hands over his face. Covering the face with our hands is a behavior which is known as a blocking technique, which is performed when faced with something that causes us great distress (as seen in the earlier analysis during the Oprah interview, when she questions him for details about his childhood). This behavior derives from our limbic system, which is an area of our brain that reacts immediately and instantaneously to threats around us. Our limbic responses are responsible for the freeze, flight and fight responses that are hardwired into all homosapiens. Michael here was clearly wishing to vanish away from this situation, hence the blocking behavior being favored.

This type of evasive 'blocking' behavior was performed unconsciously without thought, and gives us a true indication as to Michael's inner feelings towards this question. This behavior can also be seen where disbelief is present, and I feel this could be the reason why Michael performed this immediate blocking mechanism, as he wished to create a substantial physical barrier between himself and the interviewer's offensive question.

Michael's use of the blocking gesture also shows me that he wasn't concerned about trying to make a convincing impression on the interviewer, and his immediate emotional response was a genuine display of true emotion. "*Liars tend to control their behavior in order to avoid giving away possible nonverbal cues of deception and to make a credible (reliable) impression.*" (DePaulo, 1988, 1992; DePaulo & Kirkendol, 1989; Ekman, 1989; KOhnken,1990).

What is also worth mentioning is how Michael's head shakes from side to side for approximately 8 seconds after he is asked if he had ever molested Brett Barnes, which serves to strongly reinforce his denial. This is consistent with his other non-verbal responses of disbelief. The fact that Michael has so far shown surprise, anguish, face-hiding behaviors and subconscious head shakes are reliable signs that he hasn't committed the acts in question.

Interviewer: *Do you know a person by the name of Macaulay Culken?*

Michael Jackson: *Yes.*

Interviewer: *So you are allowed to answer questions about Macaulay Culken?*

Michael Jackson's attorney: *I'll let him* (i.e. Michael) *answer that one.*

Interviewer: *To your knowledge, Mr. Jackson, were you ever accused of having sexually molested Macaulay?*

This question triggers disbelief in Michael, and for the first time in the interview, anger is becoming apparent in his non-verbal responses. He begins by tightening his lips and pressing his eyebrows down and together and he again shakes his head '*no*' at the same time - behavior we have seen before and which is a reliable indicator of disbelief. Michael then makes a slight hat grasp movement with his right hand that could be described as a displacement behavior - these actions can be done to relieve stress, as '*displacement activities are small, seemingly irrelevant movements made during moments of inner conflict or frustration'* (Morris, 2002: 266)

However, what happened next in the interview shocked me, as I wasn't expecting such behavior to feature. Upon shaking his head '*no*', we see a body language display which is indicative of arrogance. Michael begins to interlock his hands behind his head and pushes his head back. This display is normally seen in the workplace, where a boss may use it to show their dominance over their subordinates. When I saw Michael make this particular gesture, it caught me off guard, as this display didn't correspond to the rest of the behavior he had previously displayed. Joe Navarro calls this posture a '*hooding*' display, because it resembles a Cobra which "*hoods*" to alert other animals of its superiority (Navarro, 2008, 124).

Perhaps Michael was making the '*hooding*' display because he had such confidence in his innocence, knowing that the evidence in this case would prove him to be innocent. The justice system is in place after all to protect the innocent and punish the guilty. In terms of the accusations made in this interview, Michael later settled out of court, but it is interesting to note that the grand juries questioned over 200 witnesses, but Jordan Chandler's claims could not be corroborated. Furthermore, there are rumors on the internet (which cannot be verified) that Jordan has since admitted that he lied about what happened and that his father forced him to make a false accusation against Michael.

Whilst making this superiority display, Michael presses down his eyelids tightly for approximately 3 seconds, which again is a variation of behavior we have seen before from Michael. This '*eye block*' is done without using the hands, as they are busy making the superiority display. The message the eyes are sending out contradicts the arrogant display his arms are making. The arm display is shown when confidence is high, but the tight compression of the eyelids reveals inner distress and disgust at being accused of such indecent conduct.

Michael continues with this arrogant '*hooding*' display, and then proceeds to make another behavior which caught my attention - he briefly protrudes his tongue out of his mouth whilst smiling. Research has indicated that tongue displays can be linked to the '*duping delight*' that liars feel when their lies are being believed. "*In social or business discussions, this tongue-jut behavior is usually seen toward the end of the dialogue, when one person feels he has gotten away with something and the other party has failed to detect or pursue the matter. If you see tongue-jutting behavior, ask yourself what just transpired. Consider whether you may have been fooled or cheated, or that you or someone else just made a mistake. This is the time to assess whether someone is putting one over on you."* (Navarro, 2008, 195)

After closer inspection, I think the footage actually shows Michael biting his tongue briefly rather than actually jutting it out of his mouth, as I don't believe that it was his intention to dupe anyone. This tongue-biting is significant because one could surmise that he is actually physically stopping himself from having an angry verbal outburst that he may later regret. After the tongue display, Michael continually grins which may again indicate his supreme confidence in his own innocence (he is almost laughing off the accusations).

Another interesting point about tongue protruding behavior is that it plays a role in social avoidance. Pioneering Zoologist Desmond Morris has identified that small children often protrude the tongue when they wish to be left alone – *"Ob-*

servers noticed that nursery-school children protruded their tongues slightly whenever they wanted to avoid a social contact. If they were busy doing something and suddenly it looked as if they were about to be interrupted, out would come the tongue." (Morris, 2002, 68)

Michael continues to silently reveal his disbelief, and consequently changes his locked hand position from the arrogant interlocked *'behind the head'* pose to placing them securely on his head. This behavior might seem innocuous, however it is quite significant as it is continuing to show a silent message that he can't comprehend the nature of this Police interview. Placing your hands directly on your head corresponds to the message of disbelief, and as his head pulls back, he is almost looking to the heavens for salvation. This type of characteristic behavior can be witnessed at many football matches where the home team misses a last-minute penalty.

Michael is then asked if he recognizes the handwriting on two sheets of paper in front of him; he says he does, and proceeds to say that it's his handwriting. He is then asked if he knows what these documents are and he replies that they are crazy stories that people have created, things he wanted to set straight in an interview. Michael continues and states that if people hear a lie long enough, they start to believe it. Michael here uses baton signals, which are subconsciously employed to emphasize key points during a statement. Morris (2002:78) states that baton signals *'beat time to the rhythm of spoken thought. Their essential role is to mark the points of emphasis in our speech'* These can be seen here through the rhythm and intensity of the head nods he makes during this section of the interview.

Michael's demeanor here has now totally changed from that seen at the start of this interview. Before, he showed his discomfort by using blocking behaviors, however in this section, his manner has changed. Now we see him swiveling slightly on his chair as he talks, which illustrates his newfound comfort in the situation (he is noticeably growing in confidence as the interview is progressing).

The next section is quite a significant part of this interview, as Michael talks about the many myths and lies about his life and personality. When he talks about whether he bleaches his skin, Michael uses a very emphatic and pronounced corresponding negative head shake. Often, when people aren't telling the truth, they can make a gestural slip, actually nodding slightly when saying no: "*While typically involving more subtle than exaggerated head movements, this incongruity of verbal and nonverbal signals happens more often than we think. For example, someone may say, "I didn't do it," while his head is slightly nodding in the affirmative*" (Navarro, 2008, 217). His verbal rate in this section noticeably increases which shows that he is comfortable discussing in detail what he perceives to be fabricated stories. One must argue that if he knew that these stories were actually true, then he would be showing non-verbal signs of discomfort when discussing them, instead of the more confident signs as already discussed.

We again see the same behavior (subconscious head shaking) that we saw previously in the Oprah interview when Michael talked about how the media has suggested that he wanted a '*white kid*' to play him as a child. However, there must be an exception to every rule, and non-verbal analysis is no different. We see in the next section that Michael emphatically states that he's '*not gay*', but proceeds to nod his head 'yes' as he does so. After watching this in real time, I was quite surprised at this behavior, however I feel that if Michael was in fact subconsciously revealing that he was gay, his facial expression would have changed during that statement. His face shows the same expression from the start of that sentence to the end, showing that no intention is being made to dupe the interviewer. This is just another example of how body language isn't always the same for everyone; idiosyncrasies play an essential role during people-watching. There are limitless variations on what behaviors we can perform, and this contradictory signal of verbally saying *'no'* but nodding the head *'yes'* is a fine example of how confusing reading body language can be. In addition, it is an example of what Ekman describes as the Brokaw hazard (1985:91), which is where an observer can misinterpret a person's body language as reflecting their guilt, when in actual fact what they have just witnessed is just an idiosyncrasy of that person. For instance, we have seen Michael in chapter two shake his head from side to side when he said he was totally innocent of any wrongdoing, therefore showing that this supposedly contradictory behavior is just one of his mannerisms and nothing more. Michael continues by saying *"Don't judge a person unless you have spoken to them one on one"* which again he emphasizes by nodding and increasing his eye contact with the interviewer. The last statement Michael gives before the end of the video is: *"Jesus said to love the children, and be like children, be youthful and innocent, and pure and honorable.*

He was talking to his apostles, and they were fighting about who was the greatest amongst themselves, and he said, whoever humbles yourself like this child is the greatest amongst me. He always surrounded himself with children, and that's how I was raised. To believe, and to be like that, to imitate that. I don't know what you're trying to make out".

Again during this section, we can see Michael is more relaxed than at the start of this interview, as he makes guide signs with his arms to illustrate the points in his statement. When Michael said *"He* (Jesus) *surrounded himself with children"* he makes a corresponding mimicking hand gesture by sweeping his hands in front of his body, to replicate the action of *'surrounding'*. This hand display is out of shot, however you can deduce that the movement occurred by looking at Michael's shoulder movement. This correlation between your words and gestures comes naturally when you're telling the truth, whereas if you are lying, it can be less synchronized. As I have previously mentioned, you don't have to think about making a credible impression if what you are saying is the truth. The interview ends with Michael saying to the police interviewer: *'I don't know what you're trying to make out.'*

Summary

This was the only segment of this particular footage that was available so I was unable to gain a complete picture of what was discussed, but I think Michael's body language spoke for itself. At the start of this interview, he was showing classic discomfort behaviors, such as blocking the face with his hands and pressing his eyelids down. What is interesting to note is how Michael flashed surprise, discomfort and anguish when asked if he had sexually molested Brett Barnes. As I have previously mentioned, these are emotions that you or I would flash if we were accused of something so offensive. In my opinion, if Michael had sexually molested Brett Barnes or Macaulay Culken, his face would have flashed fear, not surprise.

Living with Michael Jackson interview - Martin Bashir February 3rd 2003

British journalist Martin Bashir interviewed Michael Jackson over the span of eight months, from May 2002 to January 2003. It was first shown in the United Kingdom on 3rd February 2003.

The interview starts with footage of Michael walking Martin around Neverland, and what is significant is that Michael again displays the '*hands behind the back*' gesture that he used when he was showing Oprah around 10 years earlier, showing he has lost none of his sense of pride in his theme park. Martin then reveals that this interview will showcase the '*disturbing reality*' of Michael's life at present, a choice of words which already reveals his opinion about his interviewee. Martin goes on to say that in this documentary, you will see Michael as you've ever seen him before, discussing his music, money, children, sex life and face. What is immediately noticeable is how Michael's facial structure has massively changed when compared with the previous three interviews

I have analyzed; his nose, chin, eyes and expressions look noticeably different.

Martin starts the interview by asking Michael how he sets about writing a song, yet he does not give him quite enough time to formulate an answer, and as such, ends up interrupting Michael and talking over him. As this was the first question of the whole interview, it does not bode well. When Martin asks Michael how he came up with the tune for Billie Jean, he presses (indeed almost orders) Michael to give him a demonstration of how he dances. Michael is visibly shy about such a request as his hand touches the back of his head, showing that he is uncomfortable. However, Martin is persistent almost to the point of rudeness, and does not pay any attention when Michael states how shy he is. Eventually, and reluctantly, Michael agrees to a dancing demonstration. It is unclear if this is the actual opening segment of the interview, or whether this was filmed at some point and shown as the opening segment.

Michael then tries to educate Martin about the secrets of the moonwalk, but Martin has difficulty in performing it. Martin says that the Neverland Ranch is paradise for a 10 year old child, but Michael is 44 years old. Martin almost has a condescending manner when he delivers that statement, which again concerned me about the tone this documentary was going to take. I was always under the impression that journalists had to remain impartial towards their interviewees; however it did seem that Martin at this stage was beginning to paint Michael in quite a negative light.

Michael states that Peter Pan is such an inspiration to both him and the Neverland Ranch because Peter Pan represents youth, childhood, never growing up, magic and flying - the wonderment that children love. Michael then states that he is Peter Pan, which causes Martin to state '*no you're not, you're Michael Jackson*'. The reply was '*I'm Peter Pan in my heart*', and as he says this, he makes a subtle smile.

Michael then takes Martin to his '*giving tree*', and Michael uses an umbrella as he walks to protect his skin from the sun, as this aggravates his vitiligo condition. Significantly here, Martin now starts to refer to Michael as '*Jackson*', showing a lack of respect. Michael tells Martin that he calls this his '*giving tree*' because he has been so inspired whilst being up the tree that he has written many of his songs there, for instance Heal The World, Black or White and Childhood. Michael proceeds to climb the tree and invites Martin to do the same. Again here, Martin's tone with Michael is almost on the verge of condescending – *"You actually say that you climb that tree?"* – and whilst doing so, he has his arms folded across his chest. Arm folding is an example of closed body language, and it carries different meanings according to the situation. Here, I feel it is a reflection of Martin's negative attitude towards Michael's admission that he likes to climb trees. Allan Pease states that *'by crossing one or both arms across the chest, a barrier is formed, that is, in essence, an attempt to block out the impending threat or undesirable circumstances (or) when a person has a negative attitude, he will fold his arms firmly across his chest'* (Pease, 1981: 58). Morris (2002) adds to this description by saying that arm-folding can also be a kind of self-hug, used to give oneself a sense of security when feeling unsure.

Next, Michael climbs half way up the tree and Martin attempts to follow him, yet stops much further below him. Michael shouts down to Martin and asks *"You don't climb trees?"* The camera pans to Michael's face as he's sat in his tree, looking deep in thought. One could argue that climbing the tree and remaining up there away from Martin is a way of escaping from him. Again the verbal exchange between these two further highlighted my concern for the rest of their time together, because it was evident that they had very little in common and Martin was speaking to Michael in a patronizing way. Either that, or the editing of this section was done in such a way to make Michael's tree-climbing behavior '*appear*' more peculiar than it actually was.

Michael states that his two favorite things are climbing trees and having water balloon fights, to which Martin asks (quite flippantly) if he doesn't prefer making love or going to a concert. Martin here is using an aggressive head behavior to almost intimidate Michael, done by angling his head towards him which makes direct eye contact more intense. Michael says '*huh?*' which is often performed when we hear a question that we weren't prepared for (and indeed he demonstrated the exact same behavior when Oprah asked him an uncomfortable question). Michael states that some people like to play football, he likes to climb trees, and here he distinctly tightens his lips during this exchange, which is testament to my thoughts that the tension between the two seemed to be increasing. Martin's condescending attitude seems to be beginning to aggravate Michael who was reveal-ing his inner mood by showing tightened lips.

Martin says (again in a disparaging way) "*So, how had this sing-ing and dancing genius arrived in this surreal place that is his life today? I started to look for answers back at the beginning*". He asks Michael if he remembered when he first discovered that he had a special musical talent, and he tells Martin that it was when he was making his bed one day and his mother heard him singing. His mother told Joe (Michael's father) who then told his mother that Jermaine was the lead singer, not Michael. Michael here makes a direct hand gesture towards the back of his head which is most notably seen when tack-ling a stressful issue. Michael tells Martin that as soon as Joe heard his voice, he was the new lead singer of the Jackson 5.

Michael and Martin now watch the footage of Michael per-forming with his brothers in the Jackson 5, and states that throughout his childhood, he was referred to as a '*45 year old midget*' because of the way he sang and moved on stage; his behavior wasn't that of a child. Michael used this exact de-scription during the Oprah interview 10 years previously (see chapter one).

Martin then asks Michael what getting disciplined by his father was like, and Michael here looks visibly shaken, and takes his time before answering. He makes quite a distinct facial expression with his lips, stretching them wide before he answers. This behavior is especially apparent when someone is about to say something they possibly know they shouldn't. He states that he didn't have it that hard, but significantly he closes his eyes and tightens up his face in the process. If you cast your mind back to the Oprah interview I have covered, he talks openly about how his father used to beat him. Here he talks again about his father, but tries to lessen his father's actions by saying that *"he didn't have it that hard"* - but tellingly, his facial expression betrays his words. Often when we feel it's appropriate to conceal our true feelings, our facial expressions can't match our words.

Michael tells Martin that he would practise dancing while his father held a belt in his hand, and if he missed a step, he would get whipped. Michael mimics the action of being whipped and says that his brother Marlin was hit the most. Michael's facial expressions and gestures look a lot more intense during this section, and he then informs Martin that he was beaten too often by his father. Martin asks if it was just the belt he was hit with. Michael here breaks down, placing his left hand over his eyes. This is blocking behavior we have seen before during the Oprah interview and is used to block out our eye contact with the other person. Michael's facial expression is one of anguish, and this feeling is made more apparent as he makes a palm thrust gesture towards Martin and the camera in an attempt to block them both out, because he wishes to be left alone (as he's very upset). Interestingly, when Michael breaks down and cries, Martin makes no attempt to show him any sympathy, showing a lack of empathy. Indeed, what he actually does is he asks Michael what else he was hit with. Michael then tells Martin that his father also used to hit them with ironing cords and threw him up against a wall as hard as he could. He tries to explain more, but Martin keeps interrupting Michael mid speech, again showing a lack of both empathy and respect.

Michael says that he remembers (whilst his father was attacking him) that his mother screamed '*Joe, you're gonna kill him! You're gonna kill him! Stop it, you're gonna kill him!*' and as he does so, he again makes the '*hand to the back of the head*' gesture. This appears prevalent when he is discussing something he finds distressing, so one could argue that it is a self-comforting gesture. He is smoothing his own hair, almost like an adult would do to comfort a small child, because "*the stroking hand rekindles the sensation of a parental caress*" (Morris, 2002,145). He tells Martin that he was fast, so his father was often unable to catch him, but during the times that he did catch him, the punishments were severe. Michael again places his hand behind his head, which further emphasizes his anxiety whilst talking about this sensitive issue. Michael tells Martin that they were all terrified of their father (meaning himself and his brothers). Michael now repeats what he told Oprah in 1993 that he used to be physically sick with fear in his father's presence. He tells Martin that he strongly hated his dad for beating him, and it's the reason why he doesn't lay a finger on his children, because he doesn't want them to hate him. Michael states that he wasn't allowed to call his father '*Daddy*', saying that he had to call him '*Joe*' instead. Here he makes an angry facial expression when he mimics his father's words ("*I'm not daddy, I'm Joseph to you*') highlighting the anger his father had towards him. He says that he forgives his father, and makes a partial arm scissor which transmits the message of pushing away the hurt he has caused Michael. Michael then states that he doesn't allow his children to call him '*Michael*'; he's referred to as Daddy. Michael also tells Martin that when people say that the '*abused (go on to) abuse*', it's not true in his case.

The interview then moves to Las Vegas as Michael is going to spend a few weeks in the Four Seasons Hotel and invites Martin to come along.

Martin goes into Michael's hotel suite, and asks him what a mobility scooter/motorized wheelchair is doing in the room. Michael tells him that he uses it when he's bored and rides up and down the hotel corridors on it at night. In response to this, Martin's facial expression is one of incredulity and he laughs in disbelief at this admission. Michael is then seen playing on a loud simulated video game (that requires him to continually make the action as though he was on a skate-board) wearing what appear to be pajama bottoms; Martin is standing watching, with his arms folded and wearing quite a negative facial expression. It appears that he cannot quite take on board such apparently odd behavior from a global mega star. Again, the tension between them is becoming increasingly more apparent, and Martin is further conde-scending towards Michael by saying "*I wouldn't like to see you drive a car"* with reference to his ability to control the skateboard whilst playing the video game.

Next, Michael sits down with Martin who tells him that during the Jackson 5 tour, he had to sleep in the same room as one of his brothers, and on a few occasions, he had to pretend to be asleep as his brothers would bring back girls into his bedroom. Michael said that he heard his brothers having sex with the girls, which embarrassed him. Michael tightens his lips and wrinkles his lower chin, which again both remind us of his frustration at having to discuss this very uncomfortable and embarrassing subject matter.

Michael states that he didn't have many girlfriends during his adolescence, and says the first girlfriend that he loved a lot was Tatum O'Neil. If you cast your mind back to the Oprah interview, this could be the *'other girl'* he said that he loved. Michael says that he wasn't ready for some of the things that she had in store for him and when Martin asks what exactly he meant by this, Michael makes both an eye block and a lip tightening gesture, which show his discomfort (a repeated behavior for him). What is noteworthy is that a grown man with three children should be so uncomfortable and embarrassed discussing any sort of sexual matters, which does again highlight his child-like nature. Later, he makes a full facial block with his hands during this story, saying that he made this gesture when Tatum was trying to seduce him one night.

The interview then continues in the back of Michael's limousine, when Martin asks if he has always been good with his money. Michael says that he was getting monthly $200,000 checks in the mail when he was 12 years old and continues by saying that he used to be given a certain amount of money a month by his father which he would spend on sweets. Martin presses Michael into revealing how much he is worth; Michael is hesitant at first and makes a forced smile, but reveals that he is worth over $1 billion. What is also interesting is that when pressed to reveal this private information, he raises his shoulders up in a manner known as the turtle effect. This is where the head hunches downward and the shoulders are raised up, as the person almost wishes to appear smaller and hide, like a turtle retreating into its shell at the first sign of danger.

Martin arrives at Michael's favorite shopping centre, and Martin says that Michael wanted to spend some 'serious money' here. As Michael is walking into the shopping centre, he is stopped by man who says he's a big fan. They greet with a handshake and the fan proceeds to hug Michael, who reciprocates. This exchange shows us that despite his mega stardom, he is still humble enough to take the time to speak in a friendly manner to a fan.

Michael then points out to Martin the magnificently designed ornate ceiling, yet Martin's disparaging response was to ask if Michael thinks that it looks '*tacky*'. Michael's response had a tone of disbelief: '*are you silly?*' It almost looks like Martin is criticizing every aspect of Michael's life so far, which Michael is beginning to tire of. We can see this because Michael interrupts Martin at this point, which is unlike him. Martin was asking him a question about Elizabeth Taylor, but Michael talks over him and begins to discuss that he would buy jewellery for a girl he liked but he hasn't found one he likes yet. In response, Martin again re-establishes his superiority over Michael by making yet another patronizing comment: '*there's time, you're still a young boy*'. This highlights the fact that Martin views Michael as a child and not as an adult or an equal. Michael and Martin then arrive at Michael's favorite shop, and they go round with the shop manager. Michael is pointing out things that he would like to buy, and the manager shows his silent delight by rubbing his hands together. This message has a very clear meaning, namely that *'this encounter is going to have positive consequences for me'*.

Michael continues to walk round the shop, shouting out to the manager what he wants to buy. The camera pans to the manager, who is beaming and continuing to rub his hands together. Martin asks the manager how much Michael has spent so far, but he says that he's not at liberty to say. Again, it would appear that the store manager's hands are almost glued together, as he can't hide his delight at how much Michael is spending. Martin tells the manager that he could retire after Michael has been in here, and the manager is seen to be smiling broadly and making a very smug hand restraint gesture whilst leaning on one of his items. This leaning is a territorial ownership display, which shows he has a responsibility towards the items on display. The hand gesture he performs is much like the steepling gesture Oprah used back in 1993 and signifies his superiority and enhanced status because Michael is choosing to purchase lavishly from his shop.

Michael goes downstairs and again points out which items he wants. A huge crowd has gathered outside the shop as Michael and the camera crew exit. The interview then cuts back to Michael being interviewed by Martin at The Four Seasons hotel, and Michael tells Martin (like he told Oprah in 1993) that his pimples were so bad during his adolescence that he didn't look at himself in the mirror. He tells Martin a story of how a fan recognized the Jackson 5 in an airport and wanted see Michael, who was pointed out by another fan, but then this lady said '*ewww…what happened?*' (with reference to Michael's spots). This deeply upset Michael at the time, and even when he was re-telling it to Martin, he was making lots of noticeable eye blocks, which tell us that he didn't really want to recall such a distressing event.

Michael tells Martin that his father and some of his cousins teased him about his appearance during his adolescence (he mentioned this during the earlier Oprah interview). His father used to mock him saying that he had a big nose, which must have come from Michael's mother's side of the family.

Michael again shows distress in his face as he makes a very distinct hand gesture which showed how his cousins wanted to pop his pimples, and he makes a frustrated stretched smile. He continues and tells Martin that he had to perform on stage after receiving the abuse from his father, which was very difficult to do, and states that he would have been happier to have been wearing a mask. This is an ironic thing to say, because he lived most of his life behind one mask or another, be that the media or his own personal demons from the past which affected his self confidence and prevented him from living a normal life.

Martin asks Michael what he has to say to people who say that he was a black kid and now as an adult he looks like a white man. Michael says that you have to ask God, as he doesn't control puberty or vitiligo. He then says that Martin's comment was *just ignorance* and when doing so, his eyes visibly narrowed, showing his contempt for people who make such uninformed comments. Next he tells Martin the same story that he told Oprah many years ago, about how people sit out in the sun to intentionally make themselves have a darker complexion.

Martin now asks Michael a series of questions regarding whether he's had any cosmetic surgery and lists a few, including if he's had his lips enlarged or his eyelids reconstructed. Michael states that none of it is true, and the media have created these stories; he shows more eye narrowing whilst he is issuing his denials, therefore showing his rising anger. Martin quotes one paper which said when he was growing a beard, he had each little hair transplanted into his face with a laser. Michael looks disgusted at the story, and calls the reporter who wrote the story an *'ignorant fool'*.

The camera now cuts to Martin driving and giving this commentary: *"I wasn't convinced by Jackson's explanation and felt that he wasn't being entirely honest. I knew I'd have to return to the subject of his face before we were through, but suddenly Jackson suggested a filming opportunity I couldn't turn down. The following day I would be going out on the town with the Jackson children."* Again, his use of the word *'Jackson'* to refer to a global megastar could be argued as being derogatory. The interview resumes after a commercial break with Michael and Martin in a hotel lobby. Martin meets Michael's children Prince Michael the 1st and Paris, and Michael told Martin that he never lets his children out without masks to conceal their identity. It also appears that Prince Michael's dark hair has been dyed blonde in a further attempt to make him hard to recognize, as when he had his head down in the lift, he had noticeably dark roots.

Martin comments that Michael's children were the result of his brief marriage to his dermatology nurse, Debbie Rowe. Paris is now four, and Prince is almost six. The interview continues outside, where Michael is walking with his children underneath a black umbrella to greet some fans.

The interview resumes back at the hotel room, where Martin asks Michael if he cried when Prince was born. Michael says of course he cried, and continued to state that when Prince came out he had a really big head, and as soon as he saw his head, he thought of his grandfather and brother Randy, because his head was shaped just like theirs. Michael continues and says that he cut the umbilical cord but was unable to take him home as the staff told him that they thought there was a *serious problem* with Prince, as he wasn't breathing correctly. Michael said *"Please God, don't let me have a sick child, please"* and after about a five hour wait, Prince was allowed to go home. During this section, he makes two emblems with his hands to illustrate his points: firstly, his hand touches his forehead which shows disbelief mixed with sadness and secondly, he places his hands together in a prayer-like gesture and closes his eyes slightly, which symbolizes the fact that he was asking God to help his child.

Martin asks Michael about the birth of his second child, Paris, and he tells him that she was born with her head facing the wrong way and was being choked by the umbilical cord. Michael states that he was so worried about something going wrong that as soon as he cut the umbilical cord, he snatched her and went home, still with the placenta all over her. Martin can't believe what he has just heard, and says *'You're kidding?'* and to that Michael replies *'yes, I'm not kidding... got her on a towel and ran'*. Michael seems totally oblivious to the fact that his actions towards the baby could have had disastrous consequences, but what is far more significant is that this story sounds so far- fetched that one struggles to comprehend that it could have really happened.

My first point that I want to make is that when initially asked if he was kidding, his first word was *'yes'*, which may have been a Freudian slip (implying that he IS actually kidding). One would have to question his reasons for making up such a strange and somewhat disturbing story, but one could also say that he had no real awareness of how this revelation would further enhance some people's opinions of him as being very much detached from normality. My second point is that Michael would probably have hired the best doctor money could buy in order to assist at the birth of his 2nd child (particularly given the scare he had after Prince's birth) and therefore, he would simply not have been allowed to snatch a baby covered in placenta and run off with it. This is because the placenta has to be carefully checked after birth to ensure it is intact and none has remained inside the mother to cause an infection.

He then justifies his actions by saying that Debbie and the doctors told him that everything was okay, and it was fine for him to take Paris home. Michael tells Martin that he was so afraid of the doctors telling him any bad news that he wanted to go home immediately after getting the all-clear that Paris was okay to take home.

Next, the interview cuts back to Michael with his children walking into a shop to show Martin his latest acquisition, a gold replica coffin of Tutankhamen. Martin asks him if he would like to be buried in something like that, and he responds by saying that he wouldn't ever like to be buried, and would like to live forever. One would expect that Martin would have asked for more explanation regarding this bizarre answer, but (probably due to selective editing) the film just moves on to Martin asking Michael if he tries to give his children a normal upbringing. He tells them that his children do attend a school, but not a normal school as the paparazzi are always covering their every move – his children cannot have a normal life. It is reassuring that Michael uses the pronoun 'we' when referring to his family, showing that he is protective towards them.

Martin asks Michael if he worries that his super stardom has an effect on his children's life and Michael says that it's just the way it is, and he has sculpted and molded his children's world to accommodate his stardom. Martin asks Michael about his 3rd child, Prince Michael the second. Michael responds and says that they call him Blanket because it's an expression he uses with his family and employees, meaning that a blanket is a blessing. Martin questions Michael as to the identity of Blanket's mother but Michael says that he can't say who she is, because she will be bombarded by the press (plus they have a contractual agreement meaning that Michael can't disclose her identity). However, he does reveal to Martin that she is someone whom he's had a secret relationship with and he reiterates that he doesn't want anybody to know her identity, because of the *"scumbag"* comments that the tabloids will make about her. It is interesting that, even as he said this, he hesitated between the word *'scum'* and *'bag'*. At this point, he rolled his eyes skyward and then placed his hand on his chin, in a movement that Morris describes as a *'beard scratch'* which is done *"as an unconscious action performed as a minor comfort device when wrestling with a difficult decision or complex idea'* (1994:8). Maybe he thought that describing the tabloid's comments as *'scumbag'* would have consequences or repercussions for him, which is why he performed this characteristic action , or maybe he just does not like using any type of language that is classed as being derogatory towards another person.

Martin asks Michael if any of the children's mothers live with him now, and he replies by mirroring the question back to him. This is a verbal sign of anxiety which can be viewed (alongside the many non-verbal gestures that he's already made) as showing how uncomfortable he is. Martin asks Michael if it is difficult to raise his children without their mothers present and Michael replies that many babies live with their mothers and they don't have their fathers around, and that women do play a part in their upbringing as the children are with women all day. Martin asks *"What would you say to somebody who says that's a bit strange…that none of your children have their mothers?"* and Michael replies by saying: *"People can always have a judgment about anything you do so it doesn't bother me. Everything can be strange to someone. This interview is strange to some people out there so who cares, right?"* Maybe here he is indirectly hinting about how he feels he is being portrayed during this interview.

The interview returns after a commercial break and Martin goes to meet Michael in Berlin, however as Martin was arriving, Michael had just dangled his new baby Blanket out of the window of a hotel room. Martin states that when he got up to Michael's hotel room, he was worried, as there was a manic quality about Michael that he had never seen before - and Michael was loving the attention of the screaming fans outside the hotel. Michael then proceeds to write the message '*I love you with all my heart ~ Michael Jackson*' on a hotel pillow and throws it from the hotel balcony to the fans below. The fans below are chanting '*F the press, Michael you're the best*', and what is noteworthy is that Michael doesn't actually say the F word when Martin asks him what they are shouting, he only spells it out - again highlighting his childlike innocence.

Martin says that Michael had arrived in Berlin after a week of appearances in a Los Angeles courtroom where he had to answer questions relating to child abuse allegations. Martin further states that media coverage of the court case described his face as '*disintegrating*'; an unclear statement which could have been referring to his actual face or his public persona. It appears that this section has been edited in such a way that it makes Michael's behavior look very odd and erratic, even to me as an impartial observer, as we see him wave to the camera strangely, pull a face and cover his face in a lift.

The interview continues inside Michael's limousine with Martin asking him what he thinks of the press coverage of the court case. Michael says that he hasn't seen any of the case because he doesn't watch TV or look at the tabloids.

He states that the media sensationalize and that there should be a tabloid burning. When he says that people should be more aware that the tabloid accusations are completely not the truth, as he says *'completely'*, he further reinforces this emphatic denial by using the head baton signal that we have seen in previous interviews. The head almost beats in time to what he is saying and adds weight to his statement. Michael continues and says that his treatment by the press is like what they did to Lady Diana, and says that Diana had been hunted by the press.

The interview resumes with Michael leaving a restaurant and being chaperoned into his limousine. There is a total frenzy surrounding Michael's presence and he is seen to be attempting to collect some memorabilia that his fans are offering him. Michael holds up one of the posters he has collected: it is a photo of a small boy (a toddler) with two yellow roses. Next, one of his fans appears at the door and asks Michael if she can have a hug – he agrees and she goes inside of the limousine and they hug. This segment again shows that he is hero-worshipped by his fans and has an almost God-like status for them.

The interview continues the next morning, with Martin saying that Michael was keen to show him how he cared for his children. Michael is cradling Blanket and feeding him with a bottle, however he has difficulty in removing the scarf that is covering Blanket's face to protect his identity. Martin looks on in disbelief at Michael's feeding tactics, as the baby is clearly struggling to suckle with the obstruction of the veil. Martin's disbelief is shown through his posture – he rests his right arm on the table and uses his right hand to support his head, and in doing so, his hand almost covers his eyes as he is wanting to block out what he is seeing. With his other arm, he is making the akimbo gesture which Morris states is performed '*whenever we feel anti-social in a social setting*' (2009:187). We saw further evidence of this social avoidance gesture during Oprah's interview in Chapter One; it was used by both Oprah and Michael.

Martin asks Michael if he's heard about what people have been saying about his behavior at the Berlin hotel and he replies that it is total ignorance, and he would never try to kill any of his children. He asks why would he try to '*throw*' Blanket off the balcony when he put a scarf around him to protect him? When he says this, he is still bottle-feeding

Blanket and his feet and legs are juddering wildly, showing that he is very wound up and anxious. Michael continues and says that he was waving to thousands of fans down below and they were chanting that they wanted to see his child, and he was kind enough to let them see. He says he was doing something out of innocence, and as he says this, his jaw tightens, showing his anger at being accused of being a bad father. He appears to have no concept of the danger he put his child in, again emphasizing his child-like nature – he appears oblivious to the consequences of dangling a wriggling child over a hotel balcony.

Next, Martin states that Jackson's behavior was beginning to alarm him. Later that day, Michael took Prince & Paris to Berlin Zoo and Martin joined them. It was supposed to be a family outing, but the press were out in force as somebody had helpfully tipped them off. Michael went to see the gorillas but Martin states that he seemed to be completely oblivious to the fact that everybody but him could see that the trip had descended into chaos. Martin was helping Michael's children as they were being harassed by the press and the crowd were chanting 'F the press'. Martin says that it's hard to believe that this was the same man who he had met at Neverland. Martin got his chance to talk to Michael about his behavior on this trip later that evening at a charity auction.

Michael says that he loves the zoo and was satisfied because he got to see the gorillas, showing his apparent lack of awareness of how frightening it would have been for two small children to have been in the middle of a baying crowd. Martin asks Michael if Prince had been poked in the eye, which generated another mirroring response from Michael who says '*Did Prince get poked in the eye? No*'. One could interpret from this that Michael didn't actually realize that the child had been poked in the eye, and so the mirroring was a stalling technique to give him time to formulate an answer that wouldn't make him appear like a bad father.

He says that this level of media scrutiny has always been present since the day his children were born and as he does so, he makes a downwards illustrating gesture with his hands in front of his face to represent the media's smothering of them. Martin asks Michael if it would be easier if his nanny or bodyguards took his children to the zoo. The reply was that he couldn't allow this, and as he says this, he makes a stop sign with his left hand to show that he wants this line of questioning to stop. He also makes a very slight postural retreat, which again showcases his discomfort at this question. We have seen both of these clues to his feelings before during other interviews, so they could be construed as being his baseline indicators of discomfort. He continues to say that he couldn't take that chance in case something happened to the children, and he would rather be held responsible for that.

Martin tells Michael that he's had a tough week, with the media accusing him of being an irresponsible father. Michael then makes an emphatic illustrating hand gesture (he squeezes them together) to show that he had a very strong hold of his son and as such, the media's coverage of the Berlin balcony incident was wrong, as he was never going to drop him. Michael tells Martin that he wasn't over-excited at the time, and he again states that he just wanted to show off his baby to the screaming fans below. He cannot understand why anyone would suggest that he was about to throw the baby over the balcony.

After the charity event was over, Michael is taken backstage by security, and again is greeted by fans who wish to hug him. One lady pulls Michael into her and gives him a kiss on the lips, and she then places both her hands over her face, which is another example of the classic blocking gesture. The fan is so overcome with emotion that she wishes to hide; moments later this same fan was so overwhelmed with emotion at kissing Michael that she literally drops to the floor and sobs uncontrollably into her friend's arms. This is a very extreme reaction and it can be argued that Michael has an almost God-like status for her, and indeed many of Michael's fans have reacted in a similar way in the past after they have had physical contact with him.

The interview continues and Martin says that this was the last night in Berlin, and that Michael was being honored at an event for a lifetime achievement. Martin also commentates that Michael was extremely agitated, and for the first time, didn't want Martin's cameras focused on him. We could interpret this as a sign of Michael beginning to become concerned about how this interview was making him appear, and maybe he wanted nothing more to do with it. Michael is seen to push the camera away from his face and onto the adoring crowds who had gathered to catch a glimpse of him.

The awards show unfortunately created great embarrassment for Michael, as the commentary was all in German, and as such, he tried to enter the stage at the wrong time. Upon realizing the confusion, he had to crouch down on the steps at the side to avoid detection. This was because the first name check wasn't for Michael, but for the awards' presenter, Boris Becker, who had to almost clamber over the hiding Michael in order to take to the stage and announce his name. Martin commentated that this trip was done to seal Michael's position as the king of pop, but it had done exactly the opposite. Moments before the interview cuts to a commercial break, Martin states that there was something else that was bothering him, as back in Neverland, he had met one of Michael's friends, a 12 year old boy. The use of the words *'bothering him'* are meant to drop the hint that he knows something negative regarding Michael and this boy.

The start of the next section gives weight to the argument that Martin already had a negative bias towards Michael, which means that this interview could hardly be described as an impartial piece of journalism. Martin says that we haven't yet touched upon his relationship with children and he crucially states *"for me, perhaps the most disturbing aspect of his life story"*. One would have to argue that it is totally inappropriate to use the word 'disturbing' in this context, as we have been shown absolutely no evidence so far which has shown Michael to have anything but a positive relationship with children.

The interview then shows Michael walking through Neverland with some disadvantaged children, and then he boards a train with them. It must be emphasized that during this brief segment, at no point during his contact with the children does anything appear to be out of the ordinary in any way. It is clear from his relaxed body language and demeanor (and his lack of any discomfort displays) that he is totally at ease in the company of these children, and they are not overwhelmed by his massive stardom - as the female fan mentioned previously was. The footage then shows Michael asking for a snow cone and saying *'me, me, me'* which further highlights his child-like nature, and Martin again says in a condescending way that this visit from the children gives

Michael the chance to be '*one of them*' (i.e. a child) again for a day.

Martin commentates that he was utterly shocked to hear that children are still sleeping over at the Neverland ranch, given the fact that a 13 year old boy accused him of sexual abuse when he was sleeping over at Jackson's house. He continues to state that this accusation cost Michael millions of dollars, and yet despite this, children are still sleeping over, sometimes in his bedroom. Martin then introduces 12 year old Gavin, who has known Michael for two years, and we are told that he was dying of cancer. Martin asks Gavin (who is sat next to Michael) what makes Michael connect so well with children; he responds with a beaming smile and tells Martin that Michael is really just a child at heart and knows how children are. Martin commentates that according to Gavin, it was Michael's love and support that helped him beat cancer, and they have remained close friends ever since.

Martin asks Gavin where he stays when he comes to Neverland, and he replies by saying that there was this one night where he stayed in Michael's bedroom. He says he actually slept in Michael's bed at Michael's insistence, and

Michael slept on the floor in the room. Michael makes a point of saying that he stayed on the floor that night (by using an emphatic head gesture), probably realizing how this interview would again portray him. It surprised me at this point that Michael didn't increase eye contact with Martin, to further highlight that there was no foul play involved in this incident. Martin seems shocked at this revelation and states that Michael is a forty-four year old man, and asks what he gets out of all this. Michael has difficulty in answering this question which is shown in his numerous false starts, which occur when we are flustered about the subject matter. Michael tells Martin that it's children that inspire him to write music and poetry, as it's their innocence that inspires him. He sees God in the faces of children and loves being around them all the time.

Next, Gavin can be seen leaning into Michael, resting his head on his right shoulder, and the camera then zooms in on the fact that Michael is holding hands tightly with Gavin (it remains focused on this for longer than necessary). Some could argue that this was to make the audience question the appropriateness of a forty-four year old man holding hands with a teenage boy, therefore further giving weight to Martin's suspicions about Michael's intentions towards children.

Martin then asks Michael if it's really appropriate for grown men to have children staying in their house, in their bedroom (Martin's emphasis). Michael says that he feels sorry for them (i.e. people who hold that viewpoint) because that is judging someone who wants to really help people. He continues and says that sharing your bed with someone is the most loving thing you can do. Martin asks if there is not anywhere else where the children can sleep and Michael responds and says that the children who come to Neverland want to stay with him in his bedroom. He says that he has never invited children to stay in his room - it's done out of their choice and with their parents' permission. Gavin tells Martin that his parents were happy that he was here with Michael in Neverland.

Martin commentates that he felt very uneasy about this section of the interview, and needed to confront Michael about what he thought was his *"obsession"* with children. He continues and states that there are aspects of Michael's life that he thinks he wasn't being honest about, such as his plastic surgery and his relationship with Blanket's mother. Significantly, he emphasizes that in particular, he wanted to return to the subject of the Neverland sleepovers. He says that he needed to 'confront' Michael about these issues, and the fact that he chose the word 'confront' almost implies that he has further evidence of Michael's inappropriate behavior towards children.

The interview resumes on the topic of plastic surgery, with Martin telling Michael that his appearance has dramatically changed from when he was a child. At this point, probably because Michael is worried that Martin is going to press him on this issue, Michael makes a noticeable gulp and his Adam's apple goes up and down. As Givens highlights, a jump of the Adam's apple is *an unconscious sign of emotional anxiety, embarrassment or stress* (2002) and we could argue that Michael is experiencing all of these emotions here, as the matter of whether or not he has had plastic surgery is very personal to him.

Martin says that *even your face has changed* to which Michael immediately replies *I've had no plastic surgery on my face.* Unfortunately, straight after this, he then contradicts himself by saying that the only plastic surgery he has had is on his nose, which enables him to hit higher notes when singing. Michael then further contradicts his initial denial by saying that he has in fact had two facial operations *'which he can remember'*. The use of these exact words is an example of what McClish (2001) would describe as a phrase that indicates deception, because you would expect that a person would be able to recall exactly the amount of times they had undergone facial surgery of any kind. I believe these denials about plastic surgery are very significant, as they appear to be one of the only times that Michael (in all of the interviews I have analyzed) could be perceived as trying to hide something – either that or he knows he is saying something that is dishonest.

Martin now asks Michael to confirm that he's only ever had one operation on his face, to which the reply came *'two, as I can remember…. I've had two'*. In the middle of this reply, Michael again makes a hand gesture which reveals how uncomfortable he is with discussing this matter - his hand swoops towards Martin, showing that he wishes he could bat this question away.

Next, the camera pans back to Martin's reaction to Michael's repeated denials regarding plastic surgery, and Martin is seen to flash a brief smile. It could be argued that he finds Michael's answers amusing because it is obvious that his appearance has changed drastically since his adolescent years. A very significant change now occurs in Martin's interview style. After he flashed the brief smile (possibly out of frustration), he tries a new technique to try to elicit a confession out of Michael regarding the plastic surgery he's had. For the first time, he starts to empathize with Michael about how difficult his childhood must have been, and states that he is sympathetic regarding the way his father teased him about his nose. He then says that, as such, he understands why Michael would have wanted to change his appearance. Showing empathy is a classic technique used by police in interviews to try to prise a confession out of a criminal. As Memon, Vrij and Bull state, '*the interrogator should try to build up rapport, basically by offering them a moral excuse for having committed the offence*' (2003:59). Martin does this by giving some excuses to Michael that he may wish to use as justifications for having major facial surgery (e.g. the teasing from his father in his childhood), but unfortunately, it does not get the confession Martin wanted. From an impartial observer's point of view, the structure of Michael's face does appear to have changed noticeably throughout his life.

Michael at this point (whilst Martin is empathizing with him) reacts noticeably, showing signs that he is becoming tired and bored of the constant invasive questions. He shifts his posture (even though it is out of shot, we can see from his shoulders and the position of his arms that he grabs the sides of the chair) which makes him look as though he is about to get up and leave – to literally escape the intrusive questions. Morris says that *'when we are about to take action, we often make small, preparatory movements. These can act as clues, revealing what we intend to do, and they are called Intention Movements'* (2002:258). Michael then moves his eyes around the room to avoid Martin's gaze and one could argue this makes him look like he is trapped or cornered. He really wishes he could escape, but he is obligated to do this interview, so in essence he cannot go anywhere. In response to a stressful situation, our limbic system kicks in, which as mentioned in chapter three, is an area of our brain that reacts immediately and instantaneously to threats around us. It gives all human beings three options when faced with threats or danger—freeze, flight or fight.

Martin's interview style reverts back to being hostile again, as he now starts pointing his finger towards Michael when asking him a question that he doesn't actually finish. Interestingly, Michael reacts to being pointed at by pointing almost straight back at Martin, almost as if to re-assert his authority. Next, Martin refers to Michael's face as '*the face*' and not 'his face', again highlighting his lack of respect and rapport with Michael on this topic. It could also be argued that, when Michael himself uses the term 'the face' to describe his own face, it is an example of distancing language and implies that '*the face*' was something he had created. Martin attempts to say something at this point but for whatever reason (perhaps down to selective editing) he never completes his sentence –he just says '*I wouldn't want....*' This is significant because it would appear that Michael didn't interrupt him, as he didn't make an interruption gesture. Michael then reiterates the fact that he has just had an operation on his nose and tells Martin that the '*honest truth*' is that he has done nothing else to his face. Confirmation statements such as this one do have a relationship with deception, because the person knows that their story isn't really being believed. As such, like statement analysis expert Mark McClish says, they feel the need to use phrases like *'honest to God, to be honest, to tell the truth etc'* (2001:67). McClish also says that as soon as you hear words like these, you should *'pay even closer attention to what the person is telling you… because studies have shown that when people use these words or phrases, they may be giving you a deceptive answer'* (2001:67).

The interview then cuts to Michael being prepared for the next section of the interview. Martin tells Michael that one day, Prince told him that he doesn't have a mother, and Michael again mirrors the question back to him (*'he doesn't have a mother?'*) - a technique he has used before when he needs more time to formulate an answer. Michael has difficulty in responding to this question; he makes a series of false starts (often associated with talking about a difficult subject) and replies that she (the mother) couldn't handle it, and that she prefers them to be looked after by him. Michael tells Martin that the children he had with his wife were *'a present'* for him from her, as he often used to walk round with baby dolls because he wanted children so badly.

At this point, when Martin is questioning the fact that the children were given as a present, Michael mentions (unprompted and for no apparent reason) that *'there are surrogate mothers that do that every day'*. Michael then tells Martin that he used a surrogate mother to have Blanket and states that he's doesn't know her and she doesn't know him. He makes a hand to face gesture here - a behavior we don't often see from him – showing that he is under stress. Whilst listening to this section, alarm bells started to ring, as I was sure that in an earlier part of this interview, he said that he had had a relationship with Blanket's mother. I then found the section and re-analyzed it knowing about this apparent contradiction in Michael's account. Even an expert body language reader like Vrij argues that it is often difficult to spot signs of deception in real time and you may need to go back and watch the footage again. He says '*that the researcher can play back their* (the target person's) *behavior as many times as desired'* (2008:52) especially when you know that deception has occurred.

Therefore, whilst reviewing the footage again, I found something that I wasn't expecting to find. When asked the question earlier '*was she someone you had a relationship with?'* Michael replies '*yes'* but appears to be trying very hard to stifle a smile; a behavior often seen in children when they are lying. This shows us that, at the time, he was indeed lying about having had a relationship with Blanket's mother, as she was simply a surrogate and it is quite possible that the two never met. When he describes later on that Blanket's mother was a surrogate and the two of them didn't know each other, there was no hint of a suppressed smile, indicating that this is because he was telling the truth this time.

This is one of only two instances in all of the interviews I have covered where Michael does appear to be lying (the other was regarding the amount of facial surgery he'd had). However, he covered up the signs well because he didn't talk too much about this topic, as that would have been more cognitively demanding. Interestingly (and perhaps because of the way it was edited) Martin failed to pick up on the fact that Michael had just totally contradicted himself on the topic of Blanket's mother – something which is further compounded by the fact that the whole issue of the identity of Blanket's mother was one of Martin's *"unresolved issues"*.

Martin then asks Michael how he selected Blanket's mother, to which Michael's initial response was to say that 'it didn't matter to me, as long as she was healthy'. Yet he then contradicted himself again by going on to describe the fact that having good eyesight and intelligence in addition to good overall health were vital factors in his selection. Martin tells Michael that it is safe to assume that Blanket's mother was white, which Michael confirms to be untrue and indeed states that Blanket's mother is black. He then states that his dream would be to adopt two kids from every continent around the world.

The interview continues and footage is shown from earlier of Michael and Gavin holding hands, and Martin comments that this was easily the most *'disturbing'* moment he had seen in their last eight months together. Yet again Martin uses the word *'disturbing'* to describe what he sees, when to all intents and purposes, Michael holding hands with a child he knows well can hardly be described as disturbing (especially given that the child is a close friend and a cancer survivor). Martin asks Michael if he could understand why people would worry about children sleeping in his bedroom, and if it is really appropriate for a forty-four year old man to share a bedroom with a child who isn't related to him at all. Michael states that when Gavin used to stay over, Michael used to sleep on the floor so Gavin and his brother could have the bed. He tells Martin that he has slept in the same bed as many children, including Macauley Culkin and his brother. His voice changes in softness to imitate that of a child when he talks about how they (himself and other children) used to go up in a hot air balloon, and he tells Martin that he has all the footage of this – almost implying that he can prove that nothing inappropriate took place. He emphatically states that this behavior is very right and very loving, and is what the world needs - he makes an emphatic finger point to illustrate this. As seen earlier, Michael failed to see any consequences to dangling his son off the balcony, and here (perhaps because of his child-like demeanor), he is oblivious to the fact that a man sharing a bed with an unrelated child could easily be misconstrued by those who are suspicious by nature.

Next, Martin asks Michael if the world needs a forty-four year old man sleeping in the same bed as children, to which he deflects the question by asking Martin if he has ever slept in the same bed with his children. Martin replies by saying that he wouldn't like his children to sleep in anybody else's bed, yet Michael says that he is fine with his children sleeping in other people's beds so long as he knows that person well. He continues and states that he knows Barry Gibb very well, and that Prince and Paris can stay with him any-time, indeed stating that '*my children sleep with other people all the time.*'

Martin says that the problem with all of this is what happened, or what didn't happen, in 1993, and when he says the words '*what didn't happen*', Michael re-iterates these words and makes a pointing gesture. He continues and states that he can't discuss the court case of 1993, and he puts his hand to his mouth at this point, as if to prevent himself from saying any more. Michael showcases his anger towards this subject as he thrusts his finger toward Martin, and states that people make the association that the word '*bed*' has a sexual connotation attached to it. Michael says that during these sleepovers, he makes the children warm milk and cookies and reads them bedtime stories, which is very charming and is something that the whole world needs. Martin then states that the reason that Michael didn't go to jail was that he settled out of court. One would have to state here that Martin is again hinting that Michael was guilty by saying that the only reason he didn't go to jail is because there was an out of court settlement. Yet Michael says that the reason for the settlement was that he didn't want a long-drawn out televised court case, so he would rather settle financially than be put through that ordeal. Michael here can be seen to be making the gesture which is often seen when one is giving evidence during a court case, where the right hand is held aloft to swear that the evidence you are about to give is the truth (as if you are swearing on the bible with your other hand). This is an important non-verbal display from Michael as it again backs up his verbal denials.

The interview then cuts to Martin who commentates that he is unable to broadcast the next section of the interview due to a confidentiality agreement Michael has. The interview resumes with Michael in tears, talking about how life as a family has been broken, with parents leaving their children off on their own, without the love and support that they need, and this is destroying the world. It makes sense to suggest that the reason that Michael becomes so upset upon discussing children who have problems in their family life is because he had, by his own admission, a difficult (and perhaps non-existent) childhood where he never really felt truly loved, especially by his bullying father, so he can fully empathize with these children. He then tells Martin that he is very sensitive to children's pain, and Michael's closing words in this interview are *'if there are no children left on this earth, if someone announced that all kids were dead, I would jump off the balcony immediately, I'm done.'* One would not really expect such a surprising and strong statement from Michael and it is indeed an unusual way to end the interview.

Martin closes the interview by commentating that Michael Jackson's Neverland was his world, where his enormous wealth enabled him to do what he wanted, when he wanted, how he wanted. This has a negative undertone in my opinion, as it has certain implications that Michael's behavior whilst at Neverland may be somewhat questionable.

Summary

This interview was an overnight sensation for all the wrong reasons. As you have seen throughout this interview, Michael wanted to set the record straight about his life, his children, Neverland and other rumors that were ever-present in his life. Unfortunately, this interview didn't help Michael Jackson's image – rather it showcased him in the worst possible light due to very selective editing. From the outset, it was clear that Martin Bashir had already formulated a negative opinion towards Michael, which was apparent in one way due to him referring to Michael as '*Jackson*' during this whole interview. Michael's body language during this interview showed that he was indeed becoming increasingly frustrated at Martin's repeated questioning and unsympathetic interview style.

One area which took me by surprise though was Michael's contradiction regarding the identity of the mother of his third child, Blanket. As you will have read, Michael initially tells Martin that he had a relationship with this woman, however towards the end of the interview, he states that they do not know each other. When Michael said that he had a relationship with Blanket's mother, he can be seen trying to suppress a smile. This could be what researchers call '*duping delight*', where Michael is trying to dupe Martin into believing that statement, and is feeling delighted because his acting ability hasn't aroused suspicion in Martin. However, as you will also have read, a big revelation came later in the interview, when Michael verbally contradicts this statement by saying that he didn't know her.

Martin Bashir was accused of something called Yellow journalism after this interview was broadcast, which is a technique used to sensationalize aspects of interviews to make them appear more controversial. This interview had serious ramifications for Michael, as his public image was once again tarnished, even though at no stage was there any inappropriate behavior between himself and a child. His intention to be free of the allegations and rumors sadly gave way to even more unanswered questions and scandal. One thing I feel that is certainly worth a mention is the lack of positive press shown towards Michael during this interview. It would seem that this documentary only showcased aspects of his life that were negative or would appear 'strange' to the viewers, such as the awards' show blunder, Michael admitting that he IS Peter Pan, Michael playing video games in his pajamas and the Berlin baby-dangling incident. Nothing showcased Michael in a positive way, for instance, very little was made of him helping disadvantaged children or his generous charity work.

Michael's body language showed that he really didn't have a rapport with Martin, and Martin's off-camera commentary was quite condescending, painting Michael to be something

I feel that he wasn't. Indeed, the New York Times shortly after the show aired described Martin as having '*a callous self-interest masked as sympathy*' (New York Times, Feb 6th 2003). Michael's response to the Living with Michael Jackson interview was quoted on the CNN website, and I feel that it is worth quoting the actual statement that was issued on his behalf through a London-based press relations company .

I trusted Martin Bashir to come into my life and that of my family because I wanted the truth to be told. Martin Bashir persuaded me to trust him that this would be an honest and fair portrayal of my life, and he told me that he was the man that turned Diana's life around. I am surprised that a professional journalist would compromise his integrity by deceiving me in this way. Today I feel more betrayed than perhaps ever before; that someone, who had got to know my children, my staff and me, whom I let into my heart and told the truth, could then sacrifice the trust I placed in him and produce this terrible and unfair program. Everyone who knows me will know the truth, which is that my children come first in my life and that I would never harm any child. I also want to thank my fans around the world for the over-whelming number of messages of support that I have received, particularly from Great Britain, where people have e-mailed me and said how appalled they were by the Bashir film. Their love and support has touched me greatly.

Michael Jackson (Feb 6th, 2003, CNN online)

Take Two: The Footage You Were Never Meant to See (Martin Bashir Rebuttal Video) February 23rd, 2003

This is a-little known interview that even I was unaware of. As far as I am aware, it was only broadcast in the USA and you can ascertain that not many people have watched it because of its low number of views on a popular online video streaming website. It is important for me to make it clear that I am analyzing this video not to decode Michael's body language (as it is predominantly made up of previously analyzed footage from chapter four) but to give you, the reader, a chance to see an unbiased version of the events of the Living with Michael Jackson interview which I feel was not offered during the original interview. Once you have had full access to the facts which follow, you will then be in a more favorable position to decide whether it was fair for Martin Bashir to edit the final interview in the way that he did.

This interview was released after Michael claimed that the Martin Bashir interview I have just covered in the previous chapter was (according to the narrator of this interview, Maury Povich) a *"twisted and edited construction of scandal and innuendo, and not a true representation of the interviews that actually took place."* After researching the situation online, I found an article from the Pop Intervention Page which stated that it was actually Michael's close friend Uri Geller who originally persuaded him to do the interview. At first, Michael was very reluctant, as he was very wary of the press, but then he decided to go ahead because he was anxious to put across his side of the story and address his fans. The article then states that *'During the interviews, Bashir always complimented Michael as if he were a brown-nosed fan (so as such), Michael probably felt good about what he'd see when he tuned into Living with Michael Jackson. Michael was disillusioned and flabbergasted when he viewed the sensationalized and biased final cut'* Therefore, this interview was an attempt by Michael to repair his image which he believed had been severely tarnished by Martin, because Martin omitted to include certain scenes in the broadcast version that would have shown Michael in a far more positive light.

The narrator Maury then says that the following footage was never intended to be aired - it was shot using private film from Michael's own cameras, and during this interview (for the first time), Michael's ex-wife Debbie Rowe speaks out in public. The narration then continues as follows: "*Also, you will get to find out what really happened during the astonishing incident in Germany, hear about Michael's childhood and how he really feels about his father, and hear about the surgery that the Martin Bashir interview didn't cover. You'll hear the truth behind Michael's children and their disguises, and go behind the rumors at the Neverland Ranch and hear how they have driven a family from their home. You'll hear from the people closest to Michael, plus a surprise revelation from the man behind the interview.*"

Maury then states that Martin had full knowledge that Michael had his own behind-the-scenes cameras documenting the footage that Martin's own film crew were recording, and that it was not a secret. Maury further states that the footage you are about to see is of quite poor quality and is somewhat raw at times, but it will enable you to draw your own conclusions. He continues to say that even though Michael has given this footage, he has no control over the editorial content of this video.

The never-before seen interview starts with Martin Bashir asking Michael "*Do you think that your success has actually made people turn against you?"* Michael replies by telling him that the bigger the star, the bigger the target, and he reels off some of the rumors about him (as heard in the Oprah interview). For instance, he says that the more popular he became, the more rumors the media circulated, for instance that he was a girl, a homosexual, that he wanted to buy the Elephant Man's bones and that he slept in a hyperbaric chamber - he categorically states that none of that stuff was true. Martin (off camera) says *"I've seen where you sleep, and it's not a hyperbaric chamber."* Michael states that people would be so surprised about how normal and simple he is - an impression that was certainly NOT given during the Living with Michael Jackson interview.

Martin commentates that *"Neverland is an extraordinary, a breathtaking, a stupendous, an exhilarating and amazing place. I can't gather together words to describe Neverland"* Contrast this viewpoint of Martin's with how he described Neverland in the original interview, which we will specifically look at later in this chapter. He then asks *"What inspired you to make a home like this?"* Michael responds with a very relaxed posture, because he is sat on the floor on a cushion (not seen during the original interview). He says that it was easy to create

Neverland as he was just being himself and creating things that he loved; he was just putting behind the gates something that he never had the chance to experience as a child.

Martin asks Michael if he's had any regrets about the way his life has been. Michael reiterates (like we have seen before) that he wishes that he could have gone and played with the kids instead of recording songs when he was a child. The interview continues with previously unseen footage of the children visiting the Neverland Ranch. Maury makes it clear that underprivileged and often very sick children are brought here by the busload on a weekly basis, and whilst explaining this, he makes a steepling gesture. This shows us that he is confident about what he has just said. Next, Michael can be seen interacting with the children, holding their hands and looking totally at ease. Again, contrast this with one of Martin's statements from the original interview: 'one of the most disturbing aspects of his life so far (is) his relationship with children'

The interview then cuts back to Martin who asks Michael if one of the children had said something funny yesterday during their trip to Neverland. Michael tells Martin that a child asked if he paid for all of these attractions, and if he had any money left over. The child was amazed and couldn't believe it when he replied that he had money left over, which Michael found quite humorous. This shows how relaxed Michael is if he feels comfortable enough to laugh about something. This is in sharp contrast to the hidden anger signals we saw at key points during the original interview.

Michael tells Martin that Neverland cost over a million dollars to construct, but he feels he gets it back when he sees the faces of the children there. Martin now asks Michael if it would be true to say that he's found friendship and inspiration in children that he hasn't been able to find in adults. When asking this, Martin uses a non-accusatory style, and he doesn't allude to anything – unlike his tone in the original interview. Michael says that this is true, and that he hasn't been deceived or betrayed by children, yet adults have let both him and the world down.

Maury then directly quotes what Martin Bashir said about his trip to Neverland during an interview given on a prime time American TV show:

"One of the most disturbing things is the fact that a lot of disadvantaged children go to Neverland - it's a dangerous place for a vulnerable child to be. Now I'm not saying that I saw any evidence of Michael Jackson being involved sexually with any children, quite the contrary. But what I am saying is that children who are vulnerable should not be going into the house of a billionaire superstar where they sleep in his bed." As mentioned on the previous page, this directly contrasts with his awe-struck description of Neverland he gave off-camera.

The next part is very revealing. Karen Faye, Michael's make up artist of over twenty years, is heard discussing (during the original interview) about how Michael is often misrepresented by the media. Martin's response is:

"The problem is you see, that nobody actually comes here and sees it. But I was here yesterday and I saw it, and it's nothing short of a spiritually...a kind thing. I've said this to him (Michael) and what I wanted to convey is those two things. And what we've had the privilege of doing this week is not only talking about the musical genius but about what we saw yesterday which was incredible." He continues and says *"When Michael is talking about things that he's passionate about, it's obvious that it's in his eyes, this is what's in his heart.'*

She then continues by saying (during this interview) that it was very hard for her to imagine that *'Michael had opened up the gates, not only to Neverland but to his heart... to Bashir and I really thought that Bashir got it...'* Note how she refers to Michael by his first name yet Bashir by his second name, showing she is much closer to Michael and wishes to remain distant from Martin, who she feels has betrayed Michael.

The next part of the interview could be seen as the lynchpin. It shows an unseen section of the original interview where Karen says *'people don't usually ask these questions, and if they do, they don't make it in the papers, they don't make it in on the interview, it's all the negative stuff...*(Michael interjects here and says *'stupid rumors')* *and they cut questions out and that's why he doesn't do interviews anymore... they twist everything'*

Martin's highly significant and completely ironic reply is that *"It's disgusting, that's disgusting. Well, we aren't doing that here..."* It is ultimately up to you, the reader, to decide why Martin chose to edit the final interview in the way he did, and what his motivations were for doing this. Did he have a personal dislike of Michael and his lifestyle or was it something more than that? All I will re-iterate is my previous comment that *'controversy creates cash'*.

Next, Maury says that he has been granted access to interviews with some of the people who knew Michael best (none of whom have been paid) and they are about to reveal the truth as they see it. Debbie Rowe (Michael's ex wife) is interviewed first and the extract is shown from the original interview where Prince had said to Martin that he didn't have a mother. Debbie now says she doesn't want her children to call her mom as they are Michael's children, and she had them because Michael wanted to be a father. She continues by saying that in her opinion, some people should be parents, and he's one of them, and then she details incidents when they have been out in public together and he has been recognized, meaning they had to call security. She re-iterates that they first met each other sixteen or seventeen years ago, and that their relationship wasn't a short-term thing.

She then went on to describe how when she became pregnant with Prince, she heard that a picture of herself pregnant was worth half a million dollars. She then describes how excited and encouraging Michael was at the birth, and that he videoed it. She now begins to break down as she recalls the look on Michael's face when Prince was finally born – she said she'd never seen him that happy before. She continues and describes how they don't have a traditional family set-up but that she'll always be there for both Michael and the children. She re-iterates that contrary to popular reports, she didn't leave the children; rather they are with their father, where they are supposed to be (in her opinion).

She now hints that the reason she split from Michael is that she got tired of being hounded everywhere she went, and she'd also had enough of reading press speculation about her. She says that doing this (the interview) is very uncomfortable for her, and we can tell that this is the case through her language and demeanor. The interview now cuts to Michael who is discussing marriage (again, unseen footage) and he says that one day, he hopes to marry again but not yet as it's too soon, and that he's been through two tough divorces. He states that he's married to his fans, God and his children. Then he says that it is difficult to have a marriage when you are an entertainer, and he further adds to the intensity of this statement by placing his hand over his heart whilst saying this, as if to enhance the truth in what he's just said.

Next, the interview changes focus onto whose idea it was to cover the children's faces with masks when they are in public. Michael says it was done because he knew what had happened to Charles Lindbergh's baby (a famous American aviator whose baby son was kidnapped and subsequently found murdered in 1932). Perhaps surprisingly, Debbie then admits that the face coverings were done at her request. Next, whilst describing what would happen if the children were kidnapped, she shows a sign of becoming distressed, as her chin boss wrinkles (the area of the chin at the front in the middle). It is a reliable indicator of sadness when it contracts or engages. As the interview continues, we see Michael say '*I don't want people seeing them because the press can be very mean... I don't want them growing up psychologically crazy because of the evil things they can say to them.... That makes sense, doesn't it?*' to which Martin replies, somewhat ironically, '*yes it does, it does.*' This shows that Martin is aware of the negative effect the media can have, however he still chose for whatever reason to edit the original interview in the manner that he did.

The interview now moves on to discussing the infamous incident when Michael dangled Blanket over the balcony of a Berlin hotel room. We again see footage of Michael discussing this event with Martin, and the most significant part of this is when he says '*I was holding that baby strong, hard, tight*'. Mark McClish (2001) who has done many detailed statement analyses of people accused of various crimes says that when a parent uses the words '*that child*' or '*this child*' to describe their own child, it is a sign of detachment. When a person is describing something concerning their own child, you would expect that they would call the child by name or at least say '*my child*'. Ask yourself how you would refer to your own child if, for instance, someone had accused you of playing too roughly with them – you would most certainly use their name or at the very least say '*my child*'. It is open to speculation as to why he chose to refer to Blanket as '*that baby*'.

The interview then also asks both Debbie Rowe and Elizabeth Taylor about the baby dangling incident, and they both corroborate Michael's version that he had a very tight hold of the baby. Neither of them acknowledge that the child was in any danger, but I would argue that holding a wriggling infant no matter how tightly over a balcony is always going to carry with it the risk of dropping the child.

Next, Maury states that on prime time TV, days after the Living with Michael Jackson interview aired, Martin stated that Michael's children were '*restricted...and overly protected....I was angry at the way his children were made to suffer*'. Contrast this with some previously unseen footage (edited out of the original interview) which showed Martin saying '*one of the things that I noticed about you over the last year is your relationship with your children, and I have to say to you that I didn't know you before and you haven't put on a front, but your relationship with your children is spectacular. And in fact, it almost makes me weep when I see you with them, because your interaction with them is just so natural, so loving, so caring, and everyone who ever comes into contact with you knows that*'

This is a totally different viewpoint than Martin portrayed in the original interview, when he described Michael's relationships with children (not necessarily his own) as '*disturbing*'. In the final section of this part of the interview, Michael describes his relationships with animals, and it could be said that he finds relationships with animals and children to be easier than those with his fellow adults, because Michael himself said that they don't judge and don't ask questions — all they want is love.

The interview continues, and Martin and Michael are discussing the events at the Zoo. Martin complains to Michael that it took three and a half hours to get in and out, yet they only spent four minutes looking at the gorillas. He also describes how Prince was hurt with an umbrella during the trip, and after Michael admits that this did happen, he makes a slight tongue protruding gesture, which is a sign that he is uncomfortable discussing this subject matter (see earlier quote from Morris 2002). What is interesting is that in the original Living with Michael Jackson footage, Michael denied that Prince got poked in the eye, however here, he admits that he was injured in the chaos of paparazzi and fans who had gathered at the Zoo.

Martin in the original footage was very clear in his narration to emphasize that this was not a suitable outing for two young children, however what he failed to mention in the original version is that Michael had been told by the staff at the Zoo that the park would be closed to the public (yet the gates were left open and fans streamed in). This misunderstanding was not explained at all, so as such, it gave the impression that Michael had willingly put the safety of his children at risk simply to spend a few minutes looking at gorillas (which was not the case).

The interview then resumes from a commercial break with Maury saying that Michael's family members are going to have a chance to respond to some of the things that were discussed in the original interview. We then see Michael's father Joseph Jackson saying *"we don't like some of the things that are being said out there"* but what is more interesting is his posture on the chair and also his wife Katherine's body language whilst he is speaking. Firstly, he interlocks his hands together whilst speaking as a restraining gesture, showing his strong belief in what he has just said, and his elbows are placed on the arms of the chair. This is done to show his confidence, as it has been proven that when we are confident, we spread out our bodies. Secondly, when Joseph speaks, Katherine lowers her head and looks downwards. It would appear that she dare not contradict what her husband is saying; she looks subservient to him.

It then cuts to Martin telling Michael that he doesn't seem to enjoy his success or wealth. Michael responds by saying that he enjoys it behind the gates of Neverland and that missing out on his childhood still affects him to this day. He says that he was very lonely, and used to walk the streets looking for people to talk to. Whilst admitting to this, he was trying hard to suppress his tears, and indeed hides his lip when attempting to do so.

Michael's father Joseph now speaks, saying that in the early days, Michael had his brothers to play with, and goes on to state that Michael used to buy candy for the other children. Michael tells Martin that the people who he knew during his childhood only spoke to him about his music and his value as an entertainer, not about normal childhood things. Michael says that he feels lonely when he's in his hotel room when thousands of fans are chanting his name from down below, and he also feels trapped because he can't go down to them. Michael tells Martin that he's not complaining as this comes with the territory; however there is some truth in the rumors that he was different because he couldn't do normal things owing to his fame. He ends this section by saying that he has been called strange and weird before, but that he is almost forced to be different, as he cannot do things that normal people can do because he is mobbed wherever he goes.

Michael's brother Jermaine now says that he can do the normal things like shopping, but that Michael cannot. Michael says that he does wish that he could do the everyday things, but he can't because every place stops for him, which is why he loves using disguises. One of the disguises he used was a mask from his music video Ghost and he describes that he once sat on a bench in Disneyland wearing it and watched people walking past him.

Michael then tells Martin that he used to hide from his father. Joe says that one thing he could see from the original interview was that Martin Bashir was trying to pin something on him, showing him to be real brutal. He says that they (the children) didn't get beatings but got '*whippings*' instead. Jermaine says that he was disciplined in such a way that was the style at the time, and he thought that having a strict upbringing was great, because it allowed them to become what they became. Michael's mother Katherine says that Joseph didn't beat them, but disciplined them with love, and states that the Bible says that if you love a child that you will discipline them. Some could argue that this is almost a justification for hitting their children.

Michael says that his father was a genius, and if he hadn't been treated in such a way he wouldn't be the person he is today. This very revealing statement was omitted from the original interview, which instead focused on the fear and anger he felt towards his father.

Next, Debbie says that Michael would never do anything inappropriate with a child - it's the furthest thing from his mind. Katherine says that he was lonely at first after the (sexual abuse) allegations, and that, despite the allegations, he never stopped loving children. Karen (Michael's make up artist of 20 years) then says that the Bashirs (of this world) will come and go, but Michael will live forever.

Michael then says that the lies hurt him the most because there are children out there who have to hear that crap. Martin asks *why people do that (i.e. make up lies about you) when all you have done is made some of the most beautiful popular music - why do people want to judge you?* Michael answers that it may be because of the jealousy of others towards his fame. One cannot miss the irony in what Martin says in this section, as his original interview with Michael was described by many as an extremely judgmental piece of television, deliberately edited in a biased way to portray Michael as a highly unusual, eccentric man who had an unhealthy interest in children.

Maury states that once again, Michael's private life was headline news due to the interview, especially because of his relationship with Gavin (the child previously mentioned in chapter 4 who had befriended Michael). Maury gives some background to the circumstances surrounding how the friendship formed between Michael and Gavin in the first place – Gavin had been diagnosed with cancer and given 3 weeks to live and one of his last requests was to meet Michael. Michael granted this wish and befriended the boy, who subsequently made a full recovery (attributed in no small part to the influence of Michael). However, how the relationship between Gavin and Michael was portrayed in the Living with Michael Jackson documentary is quoted as being a great source of concern to Gavin's family, who admit here that they had to go into hiding after the interview was aired because of all the tabloid requests for interviews.

A particular bone of contention for his family was the emphasis that Martin placed on the fact that Michael shared his room with Gavin, a fact that prompted Gavin's mother to release the following statement: 'I am appalled at the way my son has been exploited by Martin Bashir. The relationship that Michael has with my 3 children is a beautiful, loving father/sons and daughter one... to my children and me, Michael is a part of our family.' In addition, she stated that she is considering taking legal action against Martin for including Gavin in the documentary without her consent.

The next part of this interview discusses Michael's plastic surgery, and the most significant revelation is the fact that in the original documentary, the part where Michael states that he was severely burned was never shown. This is noteworthy because had it been included, the viewers would probably have had more sympathy for him in terms of his reason for having surgery. One would have to wonder why Martin chose not to ask Michael at all about this major incident in his life which affected his appearance afterwards. The whole of his hair and scalp caught fire during a pyrotechnic display that went awry as part of a commercial he was filming for Pepsi in 1984. He suffered both second and third degree burns and had to endure skin grafts to repair his scalp. The next part of the unseen footage shows Michael becoming annoyed (and finger pointing) at Martin's continual probes about plastic surgery, as he was asking such questions as 'have you had your cheeks done, have you had inserts?' Michael's reply was very ironic, as he said '*can we get past all this plastic surgery garbage?...this is tabloid stuff...come on, you're beyond this, you're a respected journalist*'. The final cut of Living with Michael Jackson can hardly be described as the work of a respected journalist.

The final part of this unseen interview focuses on the lack of objectivity seen in the original footage. It recaps the highly contradictory statements (that I've already discussed) made by Martin, such as those regarding Michael's relationship with his father and his children, his plastic surgery and his Neverland ranch. Maury then asks the viewers why the traditionally-reclusive Jackson would agree to open up and give such an intrusive interview. He then says that the compliments given by Martin to Michael throughout the interview may explain this. We then see some more unseen footage of Martin praising Michael, saying such things as '*eventually when you talk and you say it like it really is... you just light up. It's about bringing out what you're about*. Obviously, when Michael watched the final version of Living with Michael Jackson, he would have been expecting to see this praise of him being included. Instead, for whatever reason, it was never shown, and nor were many of Martin's more positive statements about Michael, his family and his life.

Summary

This has to be the most interesting interview I have analyzed in terms of revelations. It truly was an opportunity for Michael to turn the tables on Martin, and Michael must have been extremely grateful for the fact that luckily, he insisted upon having his own camera crew film the interview alongside Martin's. Had this not been the case, then Michael would have had no evidence to contradict the controversial version of the film that the world saw. Based on the evidence seen in this interview, one can argue unequivocally that Martin did not broadcast a balanced, fair and just version of Michael Jackson's life; instead, most probably to create controversy, the final broadcast version was biased, one-sided and very condescending. I fully understand why

Martin was accused of yellow journalism which was very unprofessional on his behalf.

There were many ironic statements made by Martin during this interview, but the most staggering of which has to be his reply to Michael's complaint that the media twist things – Martin says "*It's disgusting, that's disgusting. Well, we aren't doing that here...*" The original Living with Michael Jackson interview is a prime example of how selective editing is a powerful thing, as it can make people appear to be something that they are not. A clever use of tone of voice on Martin's behalf and editorial tricks such as zooming in on supposedly significant things (e.g. a prolonged shot of Michael holding Gavin's hand) can lead the viewing public to misinterpret the situation and wrongly form the opinion that something suspicious is taking place.

I feel it is also relevant here to discuss a televised statement Martin Bashir made once he heard about Michael Jackson's death in June 2009. He stated:

'...*certainly, when I made the documentary there was a small part of that which contained a controversy concerning his relationship with other young people, but the truth is that he was never convicted of any crime - I never saw any wrongdoing myself and whilst his lifestyle may have been a bit unorthodox, I don't believe it was criminal, and I think the world has lost the greatest entertainer that it's probably ever known'.*

(Friday 26th June 2009, BBC News)

One could argue that the fact he chose to justify the content of his own interview with Michael during a statement designed to state his shock about Michael's untimely death shows somewhat of a guilty conscience on Martin's behalf.

Final Thoughts

Looking back at the interviews I have analysed in this book, there is an area that really stands out, and that is how truthful Michael Jackson is. There are only a couple of areas throughout this book where I feel he hasn't been totally truthful (such as regarding the plastic surgery he's had on his face and his relationship with Blanket's mother), however when lewd accusations were made against him, you can see that his body language is emphatically denying such claims.

In the first interview I covered, you could see how the initial rapport between Oprah and Michael was lacking, and as such, Michael closed his body language off. Like I have addressed at numerous points in this book, when we feel threatened by something, we instinctively want to create a barrier between ourselves and the threat. Our arms and legs provide adequate shields for our insecurity to hide behind. Again, at one point during the Oprah interview, the seating arrangements meant that Michael was left standing, which as I've previously mentioned, demoted his status and meant he was left looking like a reprimanded child. As that interview progressed, the relationship between the two did improve, however Oprah's intrusive questioning made it difficult for Michael to achieve comfort and therefore open up to her about the sensitive issues that she wanted to discuss.

The second analysis was Michael's statement from his Neverland Ranch, and again you can see in his actions, facial expressions and gestures that he was suffering greatly from these accusations. Michael repeatedly denies any wrongdoing, and makes very emphatic head shakes and arm signals that reinforce his message. Anger and sadness are two emotions that feature heavily during this interview. As I've previously mentioned, there is nothing during this interview that raises a red flag in terms of body language contradictions; Michael is emphatically stating his innocence both on a verbal and non-verbal level, and I see no signs that he is being anything other than completely honest.

The next interview was the police interview, which I must stress again generally shows Michael being honest in his verbal and non-verbal replies. One must not forget that this interview has been edited and we only see selected segments of the police footage, but the footage we do see shows Michael registering complete disbelief at the accusations.

The final two videos really showcased Michael in a totally new light. Martin Bashir's Living With Michael Jackson interview was edited so that Michael's life was distorted, and the footage was manipulated in such a biased way that the audience were led to believe that Michael was a chaotic and strange individual who had a disturbing relationship with young boys. A point worth making is that, when we feel we are being watched (as Michael was by Martin) we never behave in a manner that is *'normal'* for us. This is described succinctly by Morris in his book The Human Animal when he states that *'only if (people) are left alone in their normal world do people behave in a spontaneous and natural manner'* (1994: 9). As such, Martin was never going to be able to showcase what Michael was really like as a person during the Living with Michael Jackson film.

Thankfully Michael had his own cameras rolling which documented the interview, and showed Martin to be full of praise towards Michael, his Neverland ranch and indeed his relationship with his own children - something which certainly wasn't seen during the original interview. The piece de resistance was of course when Martin replied to Michael's complaint that the media twist things by saying '*It's disgusting, that's disgusting. Well, we aren't doing that here...*" This is a staggeringly ironic statement given the one-sided version of the interview that was broadcast. All of the above demonstrate manipulation on Martin's behalf, and as already mentioned, it is up to you the reader to decide upon his motivation for taking such a negative stance towards Michael in the final interview.

The vast majority of the interviews that I have covered in this book showcase Michael's responses to the sexual abuse allegations, and I'm pleased to report that I see no signs that he was being deceptive about his intentions with children. Instead, my book has uncovered further evidence that the Living with Michael Jackson interview was, as Michael himself described, nothing more than a '*salacious ratings chaser*' and '*sensationalized innuendo*' (The Guardian online, 7th Feb '03).

However, Michael was so much more than a man defending his integrity against these accusations - he was a devoted father of three children. This brings me to the next media scandal, which I may cover in a future book. Some media sources have questioned the paternity of Michael's daughter, Paris. In August 2009, Mark Lester (the former child star of the hit film Oliver!) gave a video interview to the News of the World stating that he would be happy to take a DNA test to prove he is Paris' father, as he believes there to be a strong likeness between Paris and his own daughter, Harriet. Also, I have not covered Michael's brief marriage to Lisa Marie Presley, and in addition, at the time of writing, the UK press had announced that Michael was in very poor health (both mentally and physically) during the rehearsals for the This Is It tour. Legal wranglings continue to this very day, because Lloyds of London is attempting to void a £11million cancellation policy which was taken out by the show's promoter AEG. And finally, what about the tragic events leading up to the untimely death of Michael and the fact that it has been claimed in the Summer of 2012 that Katherine Jackson has lost custody of Michael's three children? All of these areas may be covered in my future writings.

By no means is this book meant as a comprehensive guide to body language, but rather the aim was to show you that Michael Jackson was fundamentally no different to you or I in terms of his non-verbal behavior, as he has experienced emotions we all commonly experience as a race: anger, sadness, happiness, frustration, disbelief and embarrassment. Body language is without doubt open to interpretation, and it certainly doesn't hold all the answers. However, I do hope that my findings have not only reinforced the belief that Michael Jackson did not have an inappropriate relationship with children, but that they have also made you more aware of not only your own body language during your daily life, but also that of your friends, family and work colleagues too. Indeed, as Morris states *'with our human body language, we are all creatures of habit. Unless we are drunk, drugged or temporarily insane, we stick to a remarkably fixed set of personal body actions that are as typical of each of us as our fingerprints...(and) for each of us, our body language is like a signature'* (1994: 9-10)

Michael's death left us with many more questions than answers, but his body language during these interviews ultimately showed the world that he was indeed innocent of all the disturbing and lurid accusations regarding child abuse, and furthermore, much like his alter ego Peter Pan, he has proven himself to be child-like in both his verbal and non-verbal responses.

I hope the evidence I have presented in my book will prove Michael's doubters to be wrong, as there is an overwhelming body of evidence that shows Michael to be innocent in every sense of the word.

The man behind the mask has finally been revealed.

Body Language Terminology

Arms akimbo – Arms placed by the side of the body, used to show that there are issues present.

Baseline behavior – Understanding what is *'normal'* for an individual in terms of their verbal and non-verbal behavior.

Blocking gesture – Done to block out the cause of stress. Can be performed with the legs, arms, hands, eyelids or any object. When we feel threatened, our natural instinct is to create a barricade between ourselves and the cause of the stress.

Brokaw Hazard – when a person's idiosyncrasies are mis-interpreted as a sign of guilt, as the observer is unfamiliar with the person's baseline body language.

Displacement behavior - Very similar to manipulators, and are tiny scratches of the body or clothing adjustments that serve no functional purpose yet reveal inner conflict or frustration.

Distancing language – Language used to create distance from a statement. *"I did not have sexual relations with that woman"* is an example of distancing language.

Duping delight. – Where a person feels delighted at their level of acting because their deception hasn't aroused suspicion in their target. Can also be seen when a person's lies result in an innocent victim being wrongly punished

Emblematic gesture – Emblems have a precise meaning, like the 'thumbs up' hand gesture. No words are necessary to comprehend the meaning of the gesture.

False starts – When a speaker makes numerous speech errors at the start of their statement – often associated with discussing difficult subjects or when a person is telling an untrue story that they haven't had time to rehearse.

Flashbulb eyes – Widening of the eyes, often seen during surprise.

Gestural slip – Gestures that contradict what's being said. A half shoulder shrug during a statement could indicate that the person knows more than they are revealing.

Gestural timing – Movements that are in synchrony with our words.

Hands behind back – Has a variety of meanings depending on context. Can be used to show how proud we are of something, that we are uncomfortable, or to show our superiority.

Hand scissors. – A chopping action performed when one wishes to '*chop*' the negativity in half.

Illustrators - Help us to exemplify our speech as it is spoken – examples would include head nods, pointing and hand gesticulations

Limbic response – This is responsible for the freeze, flight or fight response seen in humans that are facing danger. It originates in the limbic system, which is a complex set of structures found on both sides of the thalamus in the brain and supports a variety of functions such as emotions, behavior and motivation.

Manipulators – When one part of the body grooms, massages, rubs, holds, pinches, picks, scratches or otherwise manipulates another part of the body in order to dissipate stress or tension.

Mannerisms/Idiosyncrasies - A habitual gesture or way of speaking or behaving.

Micro-expressions - Very brief expressions, showing concealed emotions. Can be as brief as 1/15 to 1/25 of a second.

Postural retreat – when the body moves away from something it dislikes

Steepling – Touching the spread fingertips of both hands, in a gesture similar to praying hands. Can be used to showcase our confidence, yet overuse can make the person appear pompous.

Tightening of the lips. – Can be shown out of frustration, concealment, anger or embarrassment.

Tongue biting – Done to stop oneself from saying something that one may regret later.

Tongue protruding– Can be prevalent during moments of deep concentration, or during social avoidance.

Torso Lean. – Moving away from something we don't like. Can also be referred to as a gestural retreat.

Universal behaviors. – Behaviors that are carry the same meaning worldwide, such as crying or a shoulder shrug.

Universal facial expressions. There are seven of these and they are recognized worldwide: Happiness, Sadness, Anger, Disgust, Fear, Surprise and Contempt.

Bibliography

Bischoff, Eric. 2006. Controversy Creates Cash. Canada: Simon & Schuster.

Darwin, Charles. 1872. The Expression of Emotion in Man and Animals. New York: Appleton-Century Crofts.

DePaulo, Bella. 1988. Nonverbal aspects of deception. Journal of Nonverbal Behavior.

Ekman, Paul. 1985. Telling Lies: Clues to Deceit in the Marketplace, Politics and Marriages. New York: W.W. Norton & Co.

Ekman, Paul. 2003. Emotions Revealed: recognizing faces and feelings to improve communication and emotional life. New York: Times Books.

Ekman, Paul. 2005. What the Face Reveals: Basic and Applied Studies of Spontaneous Expression Using the Facial Action Coding System (FACS) Oxford University Press.

Givens, David G. 2002 The Nonverbal Dictionary of Gestures, Signs & Body Language Cues. (http://www.center-for-nonverbal-studies.org/6101.html.)

Gordon, N.J. & Fleisher, W.L. 2006 (2nd ed). Effective Interviewing and Interrogation Techniques. Academic Press: Boston.

Jackson, LaToya: 1990. Growing Up in the Jackson Family. Century: USA.

McClish, Mark. 2001 I Know You Are Lying. USA: The Marpa Group.

Memon, Amina; Vrij, Aldert; Bull, Ray 2003. Psychology and Law, Truthfulness, Accuracy and Credibility. London: McGraw-Hill.

Morris, Desmond. 1985 Bodywatching: a field guide to the human species. London: Jonathan Cape.

Morris, Desmond. 1994. BodyTalk: A world guide to gestures. London: Jonathan Cape.

Morris, Desmond. 1994. The Human Animal. London: BCA.

Morris, Desmond. 2002. Peoplewatching: The Desmond Morris Guide to Body Language. London: Vintage Books.

Morris, Desmond. 2009. The Naked Man. London: Jonathan Cape.

Navarro, Joe. 2008. What Every Body Is Saying. New York: Harper Collins.

Navarro, Joe. 2010. Louder Than Words: Take Your Career from Average to Exceptional with the Hidden Power of Nonverbal Intelligence. USA: Harper Collins.

Parker, Steve. 2007. The Human Body Book: The ultimate visual guide to anatomy, systems and disorders. London: Dorling Kindersley.

Pease, Allan. 1981. Body Language: How to read others' thoughts by their gestures. London: Sheldon Press.

Vrij, Aldert. 2008. Detecting Lies and Deceit: Pitfalls and Opportunities. England: Wiley & Sons.

Vrij, Aldert., Semin, G. R., & Bull, R . 1996. Insight in behavior displayed during deception. Human Communication Research.

Webb, David. 2012. Criminal Profiling (The Essential Guide To Criminal Profiling) Kindle edition.

Winston, Robert. 2005. Body: An amazing tour of human anatomy. London: Dorling Kindersley.

Websites

http://popintervention.hubpages.com/hub/Martin-basher-Living-with-michael-jackson

http://www.guardian.co.uk/news/2003/feb/07/uknews

http://www.all-about-psychology.com/

http://www.all-about-forensic-psychology.com/

http://www.all-about-forensic-science.com/

http://www.nytimes.com/2003/02/06/arts/television-review-a-neverland-world-of-michael-jackson.html?pagewanted=all&src=pm

Learn All About Body Language

If you're interested in learning more about body language make sure you visit www.all-about-body-language.com/. Here you will find free and comprehensive information (body language guides/tips/articles) along with a series of exclusive interviews with the world's leading body language experts; such as nonverbal behavior pioneer Dr. Paul Ekman who discusses his conversations with the Dalai Lama on emotional experience; his revolutionary research, the latest advancements in the field of emotional recognition; and his personal and professional involvement with the TV show 'Lie To Me'.

Connect With Me

I love connecting with people who share my passion for body language so please join me on Facebook and Twitter.

https://www.facebook.com/cjbaxx
https://twitter.com/bodylanguageuk

Questions/Comments

I would love to know what you think about *Behind The Mask: What Michael Jackson's Body Language Told The World* - so please post any questions or comments over at the book's official facebook page.

https://www.facebook.com/pages/Behind-The-Mask-What-Michael-Jacksons-Body-Language-Told-The-World

Many thanks.

Craig James Baxter

Made in the USA
Lexington, KY
08 March 2015